SHADOW MAGIC

SHADOW MAGIC

Unlocking the Whole Witch Within

NIKKI VAN DE CAR

Illustrated by KHOA LE

RUNNING PRESS

PHILADELPHIA

Running Press
Hachette Book Group
1290 Avenue of the Americas, New York, NY 10104
www.runningpress.com
@Running_Press

Printed in China

First Edition: September 2023

Published by Running Press, an imprint of Perseus Books, LLC,
a subsidiary of Hachette Book Group, Inc. The Running Press name and logo
are trademarks of the Hachette Book Group.

The Hachette Speakers Bureau provides a wide range of authors for speaking events.
To find out more, go to www.hachettespeakersbureau.com or
email HachetteSpeakers@hbgusa.com.

Running Press books may be purchased in bulk for business, educational, or promotional use. For more information, please contact your local bookseller or the Hachette Book Group Special Markets Department at Special.Markets@hbgusa.com.

The publisher is not responsible for websites (or their content)
that are not owned by the publisher.

Print book cover and interior design by Susan Van Horn.

Library of Congress Control Number: 2022952032

ISBNs: 978-0-7624-8149-1 (hardcover), 978-0-7624-8150-7 (ebook)

APS

10 9 8 7 6 5 4 3 2 1

Contents

Introduction

Think about browsing in a store, one full of T-shirts, throw pillows, water bottles, and bumper stickers. They tend to say things like "Love More," "Today Is a Good Day to Have a Good Day," "Smile!" and "Choose Happiness." And, of course, those are things we all want. We all want to be happy. We all want to have reasons to smile. We all want to have good days, and we certainly all want to give and receive more love.

But the barrage of positive messaging can sometimes give the impression we aren't supposed to feel anything *but* happy. It can seem like if we aren't happy, then we are doing something wrong or there is something deeply wrong with us. In truth, nobody is happy all the time. Not every day is a good day. And, counterintuitive as it may seem, that's actually a good thing. If we never had bad days, there would be no change and no way to determine what made our good days so good. If we were never unhappy, we would never know what it is to *be* happy. Without the darkness, the light could not exist.

So what if we could accept the darkness as good and beneficial—in and of itself? As a culture, we tend to shy away from anger, sadness, and other negative emotions that we encounter in our day-to-day lives, but these feelings can be extremely valuable. They teach us about ourselves, help us learn from our experiences, and shape us into the people we want to become. This aspect of the self that contains what we're afraid to express, or even acknowledge, is called *the shadow*. The shadow, as defined by psychologist Carl Jung, is the part of each person that exists outside the light of consciousness. When you try to ignore the shadow, it can manifest in dreams or unbidden waking moments that catch you by surprise—like when you lash out at a friend. The shadow is what regulates the unconscious, which means that by engaging with it—and with the parts of yourself that you might keep hidden—you give yourself access to more creativity, imagination, intuition, and wonder, all of which are also part of the shadow realm.

Human beings are incredibly complex. We are more than just our happiness or sunny dispositions, and we have much to offer others and ourselves even on our worst days. There is magic and energy and potential in these moments—in the shadow—and we cannot be the fullest expression of ourselves, at our most powerful, unless we embrace and embody *all* that we are.

If we can work *with* the shadow, rather than trying to suppress or ignore it, we can harness its power and bring more magic into our lives. *Shadow Magic* is here to assist you in uncovering, understanding, and celebrating your own shadow. The spells and rituals in this book will help you bring awareness and healing to whatever you may be carrying that you would rather leave behind—and it will also help you uncover your personal power, including abilities and gifts that you may not have recognized within yourself. To cultivate this awareness and healing is not to ignore the shadow, but rather to embrace what it means to be in relationship with it. You'll work with sigil magic and symbology, with tarot and candle magic, with the moon, and with dreams. Each section includes three spells for you to try: one for creativity, one for intuition, and one for self-love.

Remember, as you embark on your own journey of discovery, that shadow magic is not dark or negative. It is a part of the fullness of the self. All of your magic is carried within you, imbued with powerful potential, and available to you in all its glory and subtlety. Your magic *is* you.

Let's uncover what stirs on the other side of the light and see what kind of magic we can work if we embrace *all* of who we are, in all of our contradictions and dapplings of shadow and sun.

Light a Candle for...

Scattered throughout the book are profiles of witches from literature, folklore, and history for you to explore. These inspirational figures embraced their own shadows and, by doing so, soared with their own power.

As you encounter these witches in your reading, pause a moment with them. If you like, you can create a specific ritual that works for you. Consider lighting a candle and sitting down to read the profile. What about this witch resonates with you? Meditate on her, and consider what aspects of her you might want to embody . . . And because everyone has a shadow—even those who inspire us—what do you find yourself resisting? What shadow aspects of this witch make you uncomfortable? How can you sit with that discomfort and find inspiration within it?

Shadow magic is an ongoing practice and one that will grow and shift with your own growth and expansion.

Chapter One
THE SHADOW

The story of the *Strange Case of Dr. Jekyll and Mr. Hyde*, by Robert Louis Stevenson, can be helpful in building our understanding of the shadow and why it's important to tend to it as you would any other part of yourself. In this classic tale of two sides of oneself, the calm and composed Dr. Jekyll finds a way to unleash the part he typically represses, in the form of Mr. Hyde, who is instinctive and irrational. Dr. Jekyll does not, crucially, synthesize Mr. Hyde into his overall personality. And because Mr. Hyde has been separated from the whole self—isolating only a few of his characteristics, instead of embracing the complete complex tapestry of being— he becomes violent and takes over. When we ignore and repress our shadows, they become more negative. Ignoring your shadow does not make it go away.

Here's the thing, though: the shadow is not a demon. You absolutely do not carry some Mr. Hyde–esque rampaging murderer inside you. It's not some evil entity that invades your mind—and it isn't separate from you. It's a universal part of the self and deserves just as much care, attention, and love as every other part of you. If not acknowledged and integrated, the shadow can cause harm, but the part of ourselves that is irrational and instinctive can also be a source of good. We often think of the terms *irrational* and *instinctive* as negative—as if only conscious thought and intention can guide us in a positive direction—when the truth is that incredible discoveries await us in the unknown, in that which is inexplicable and mysterious and therefore worth exploring. That's where meaning lives, and where magic lives as well.

Parts of the Self

The shadow is just one part of you—there are lots of others, too. For the purposes of this book, we will be talking mostly about the shadow with occasional references to the other parts as they relate to integrating that shadow. But it is helpful to have a picture of the whole, even if we're only going to focus on one part. Jung defined the integration of all these various parts as *individuation*. It is how we consciously accept and welcome all of the elements that we carry within us—which is quite magical indeed. This is, of course, not something that is easily achieved or permanent—we have to continually work to be whole.

There is a lot of psychological scholarship on the various parts of the self, and it can all be helpful in your own individuation process. But for now, let's stick with Jung's four main archetypes.

THE PERSONA ✦ *Derived from the Latin word for "mask," the persona is the archetype you present to the world, much like your Sun Sign in astrology. It's an incredibly useful part of the self, as it represents how we interact with*

others. From the time we were young children, we learned how to embody our persona. Consider how we are taught to behave in certain ways to fit in with societal norms. On the face of it, that sounds bad, as though we are suppressing our truths to be accepted by society. But remember, there are no bad parts of ourselves. We learned not to pinch other children when they wanted to borrow our toys. That's a good lesson, and it is the kind of behavior and presentation that is meant by the persona, or at least an early aspect of it. As we grow up, we continue to learn how to exist among others, adapting to the world around us. That's a good thing. It helps us make friends and find community. However, as with the shadow, if we aren't conscious of it, the persona can take over and cause us to lose sight of who we are beneath it.

THE ANIMA/ANIMUS ✦ *These days, you can often find these referred to as our "feminine" or "masculine" sides. We all carry both, and the anima or animus balance our identity. So, if someone identifies as female, the animus is the masculine part of the whole. And if they identify as male, the anima is the feminine part. In our modern times, this may all feel a bit reductive,*

and frankly, psychology has come a long way since Jung, with this particular facet of the self being explored with a lot more depth and nuance. Even so, it remains helpful to recognize that we all carry feminine and masculine energies and that both are valuable, much as magic recognizes the worth of both the moon and the sun.

THE EGO ✦ *This rather famous part of the self was named by Sigmund Freud, but this definition is Jung's. (Jung and Freud were contemporaries, but they had some rather severe disagreements. Basically, Jung didn't agree that absolutely everything was about sex, and thought humans were a bit more complex, psychologically speaking.) The ego is the command center, our conscious awareness. It is the part that chooses how we relate to the external world. Typically, the ego has a bad reputation—we call people who are vain or selfish "egotistical." But the ego is just the part of us that regulates what we pay attention to and what we choose to be conscious of. That's absolutely necessary! How could we ever get through the day without*

determining what to focus on, what to give weight to, and what to allow into our experience? The thing about the ego, though, is that it's a very protective part of the whole, and sometimes it only lets in information that feels safe. This can lead to intractable beliefs and an overinflated sense of self-importance—and that's where egotistical can come in.

THE SHADOW ✦ *The shadow is in direct opposition to the ego. If the ego regulates the conscious, the shadow regulates the unconscious, though most of the time it does so, you know, unconsciously. It accepts all that the ego does not let in but tends to be much less organized about it. If the shadow isn't integrated with the whole, the persona tends to take over.*

All of these parts together make up the archetype of the self. To radically simplify Jung's theory, which is quite complex: we only develop a self when we have moved through individuation, when we have integrated all of our parts and brought them into balance with each other, with the ego as a tidy little dot in the middle.

Jung's theory is, of course, just one way of thinking about what makes you the person that you are. Magic teaches us that there are many other ways as well. We are a constellation of facets, and all of them together make us who we are. All of them are valuable.

Befriending the Shadow

Now that we have explored what the shadow is, how do we go about integrating it into ourselves and our mystical lives? One way to do this is to think of your shadow as separate from yourself—its own being entirely. But, rather than trying to excise it or punish it as Dr. Jekyll did, try befriending it instead. The next time you feel your shadow's presence, don't let your ego push it away. Bring it into the light. Jung says, "To confront a person with his shadow is to show him his own light. . . . Anyone who perceives his shadow and his light simultaneously sees himself from two sides and thus gets in the middle."[1]

You can use techniques you may already be familiar with from your magical studies—like mindful awareness—to try this for yourself. For example, when you are reacting with unwarranted anger and directing it at someone who doesn't deserve it, let that anger and its unjustness into your awareness. This may be challenging to do in the moment, but once some time has passed and you have calmed down, sit with your anger for a moment, as though you are sitting on a park bench next to a friend who is having a hard time. It won't feel good to do this. Acknowledging that you were unjust, that you were allowing your shadow to take over, can bring up feelings of shame and regret. That's okay. Letting those feelings into the light is how we can begin to change how we interact with our shadow. What caused the anger? Where did it come from? Perhaps you were triggered by memories of a past event, and you were actually angry at someone else. Perhaps you felt envious, and that feeling gave way to anger. There

1   Carl Jung, "Good and Evil in Analytical Psychology" (1959), in *The Collected Works of C. J. Jung, vol. 10: Civilization in Transition* (New York: Pantheon, 1953), 872.

can be so many reasons we behave the way we do, and it is only by doing the work of self-reflection that we can begin to act with greater intention. And intention is the root of both self-understanding and magic.

Doing this can benefit us in so many ways. If we allow ourselves access to the shadow, we can access *all* of the shadow, the positive and the negative. And as we integrate it, we can change the way we interact with the world, finding more compassion, empathy, love, and, yes, even magic.

Jung believed that befriending your shadow could change not only yourself, but also the world. So, you know, no pressure. It *is* challenging, mentally and emotionally, but so very worth it. Befriending that which you do not wish to think about, not consciously anyway, is by no means easy and certainly won't be finished overnight. It is a constant, lifelong process, and this book is not meant to be a substitute for therapy or any other form of mental health support. But the practices and spells here can complement that internal work, and even the smallest step forward can open up a world of possibility from your shadow.

The remainder of this book will explore the various positive aspects of the shadow, which your friendship with it can unlock, but the following meditation can be useful to come back to over and over again, whenever your shadow is acting unruly.

MEDITATION FOR BEFRIENDING YOUR SHADOW

When your shadow makes itself present in your life in a way that causes harm, find a way to be alone and at peace for a little while. That can mean going for a walk or a run, putting on headphones and listening to some music, or any other form of calming self-care that works for you. Once you're more at peace and able to meditate, find a comfortable seat where you can be quiet and still.

Begin by visualizing yourself. You are your body, you are the parts of the self, and you are the self as a whole. Let this fill up your entire being, then expand beyond it, as you also exist outside of your physical, mental, and emotional self. The core of who you are is more than the sum of your parts.

Once you have that knowledge firmly in your mind and heart, allow yourself to think about the moment that brought you here. Let yourself feel your anger, your hurt, and your shame. These emotions and experiences are a part of you, but they are not *all* of you. If you can, let your mind wander toward what might have brought about this reaction. Can you identify a cause or trigger? You may not be able to right in this moment, and that's okay. Just be open to whatever comes. Maybe you'll think of some amends you can make or consider how you might behave differently in the future.

Once you've fully explored what happened, hold the image in your head of sitting next to your shadow on a park bench. Imagine taking their hand, and holding it with the same compassion you would have for anyone who was hurting. Be there for them.

And then allow your shadow to merge back in with the rest of your self, whole and complete. Breathe deeply for several moments, letting your shadow settle and come to peace within you.

Light a Candle for...

LA VOISIN

FRANCE, 1640–1680

"She had as much money as she wanted. Every morning, long before she got up, [clients] would be waiting for her."

—Bastille interrogation archives

L'affaire des Poisons was a scandal that rocked the seventeenth-century French aristocracy, and a witch named La Voisin was at the heart of it all.

La Voisin was born Catherine Deshayes. From the age of nine, she began telling the fortunes of French nobility to earn enough to eat. As an adult, she married a merchant names Antoine Monvoisin, but after his businesses failed, she went back to doing what she did best: bringing magic to the French aristocracy.

She read palms, prescribed herbal remedies, and quickly grew to become one of the most powerful and sought-after women in Paris. Using the funds she received from her wealthy clients, she opened a home for unwed mothers, providing abortions as necessary and acting as a midwife, all without charge. She crafted love potions and, eventually, "inheritance powders," also known as poisons. She was not the only woman to do so—there was in fact an entire network of witches in Paris during that time.

Louis XIV, the Sun King, became terrified of poison after the murders of a pair of aristocrats that involved another Parisian witch, Magdelaine de La Grange, and sent the Paris police on a witch hunt. La Grange accused Marie Bosse, another of La Voisin's rivals, and Bosse in turn denounced La Voisin.

La Voisin was arrested, and the chief of police decided on a somewhat surprising approach to interrogation: he got her drunk. She confessed to offering her services to Madame de Montespan, the Sun King's official mistress, making love potions that Madame de Montespan used on the king and poison that may or may not have been used on one of her rivals. It came out that La Voisin, Bosse, and others had poisoned hundreds of members of the aristocracy, maybe more.

La Voisin, Bosse, and thirty-four other men and women were executed by the Chambre Ardente, the "burning court."

───◄◆►───

*While much of La Voisin's story is **not** inspirational or aspirational—we definitely shouldn't murder people—it is also the story of a poor, ordinary woman who used her power to become a force of nature at a time when the aristocracy ruled with an iron fist.*

CREATIVITY SPELL

If we aren't letting our shadow have a seat at our inner table, we aren't being our true selves completely and honestly. That can be very isolating, which is a little ironic given that we often run from our shadows to feel more likable or perhaps even more lovable. To encourage your shadow to feel comfortable with others, ask a friend or family member or anyone you trust to cast this spell with you.

Set the Mood

Anoint your wrists and the wrists of your partner with rose, bergamot, or ginger essential oils. Place some rose quartz, malachite, or green aventurine crystals nearby, and sit together at a table. Have a piece of a paper and a pencil ready.

Begin the Spell

Together with your partner, set the intention for inviting your shadows to come sit with you at the table, to participate in this ritual, and to feel welcome here. Then begin to draw with the paper and pencil. One person goes first—it doesn't matter who—and draws intuitively (i.e., just letting themselves set down whatever comes to them in whatever form). This isn't about being a good artist; it's about letting your creativity expand. Draw something, anything, whatever comes to mind, and don't worry about how it's going to look.

Pause before you've finished your drawing. In fact, pause before it's quite clear what your drawing is even going to be. Pass the pencil to the other person, and let them take over the drawing. Where does it go now? What does it become?

Often the drawing will evolve into something entirely different from what you initially envisioned. Maybe you were drawing an ocean, but it becomes a rolling hillside. Maybe your partner drew a mountain that became someone's hat. Continue to explore together in this way, having fun with it and finding out what you can create from the murky uncertainty.

When the paper is full, the spell is done. Thank your shadows for coming to play with you.

INTUITION SPELL

To draw forth your shadow's powers of intuition, this spell is going to ask you to do some challenging things. We all get in the habit of doing things a certain way—often an easier way—but sometimes it is necessary to step outside of that comfortable routine and uncover an odd or even deviant approach to our most common, everyday activities. If we let it, this can open us up to the magic of our intuition.

Set the Mood

Anoint your temples and wrists with essential oils that will augment your intuition, like lavender, frankincense, and myrrh. Gather a piece of paper and a pencil, and if you have one handy, a small mirror you can prop up. Have a seat at a table or desk, and place a lapis lazuli crystal nearby.

Begin the Spell

Choose a simple word or phrase that will invite your shadow to expand your intuition. It could be something like *welcome*, *shadow*, or *shadowfriend*, or even just *embrace*. Using your nondominant hand, write your chosen phrase three times, with as much artistry as you can—as difficult as that may be for those of us who aren't artists! Put all your intention for befriending your shadow into your writing.

Next, prop up your mirror if you have it. Don't worry if you don't—it's possible to do this part of the spell without one; it's just a little more challenging, which certainly isn't a bad thing in this case. Using your dominant hand this time (whew!), give mirror writing a try: writing so that your phrase will appear wrong on paper but correct when viewed in a mirror. Concentrate, but also keep your mind relaxed, finding the balance in between. Write your chosen phrase three more times.

Finally—and most challenging of all—repeat the three lines of mirror writing, but this time using your nondominant hand. Don't worry about not writing neatly or perfectly—this is simply an invitation, a way to expand your awareness and exercise your ability to try things in a new and slightly uncomfortable way.

When you've completed your spell, fold it up and tuck it away, perhaps leaving it by your altar if you have one or keeping it in your wallet for a little while. Let its energy permeate your life.

SELF-LOVE SPELL

This is perhaps the most valuable spell in this entire book, and also the most challenging. Learning to love your shadow is lifelong work. Casting this spell won't change that, but it can help you inch toward individuation. And if you can feel even just the breath of a moment of love for your shadow, then you are changing your entire relationship with yourself as a whole, which can only lead to more magic and possibilities in your life.

Set the Mood

Make yourself as cozy and comfortable as possible, perhaps by curling up in your favorite chair or snuggling under a blanket while holding your favorite stuffed animal, if you have one. Light a candle, and give yourself a foot rub, maybe massaging in some rose-scented oil. Take care of yourself.

Begin the Spell

Think about a moment in your past you are ashamed of. You can start with something small or if you feel up to it, revisit one of those memories that come to you in the middle of the night, the past experiences that haunt you and you never, ever want to revisit. Maybe you're remembering a time that you hurt someone, behaved selfishly, or were cruel. We all have those moments.

Put yourself back in that incident. Yes, it's painful, but remember that it's over and done with. Watch it unfold as if you were watching a movie, experiencing it as fully as you can. And then, let your memory of it expand. What else was going on that day? What can you see now with the benefit of hindsight and some space to reflect, that adds context? Were you hurting? Were you simply being thoughtless?

It's likely that you've judged yourself for this moment, but this is the time to let that judgment go. You can decide to love the person you were in that moment, not in spite of your actions, but just because you are worthy of your love.

Have compassion for yourself. Have forgiveness for yourself. Have *love* for yourself.

Light a Candle for...

RHIANNON

WELSH MYTHOLOGY, ~300 BCE

"Let us check," said Rhiannon, "that his own name doesn't best become him."

—**The Mabinogi of Pwyll**

Rhiannon is that odd combination of female archetypes commonly found in mythology—the tragically wronged, the unattainable, and the help-mate, though unlike Circe or Medea she did not wreak terrible vengeance. Vengeance was just as much a feature of Welsh folklore, also known as mabinogi, as it was of Greek, but Rhiannon somehow remained above it all.

Her taste in men left something to be desired, but she did all that she could for her chosen husband—Pwyll, prince of Dyfed. Pwyll stood atop a magical mound said to show marvels, and the marvel that appeared was Rhiannon. She rode a white horse and set off at a gentle amble. Instantly enchanted, Pwyll sent his best riders after her, but no matter how fast they rode, they could never catch her. Pwyll went after her himself, again galloping as fast as he could while Rhiannon's horse simply trotted, but to no avail. At last he called after her, pleading with her to stop and speak with him.

Rhiannon immediately stopped, chiding him for not having simply asked in the first place. She explains that she had appeared on the mound because she wished to marry him, despite being already betrothed to Gwawl ap Clud. Pwyll was delighted, and they decided to be married quickly.

At the celebratory feast in anticipation of the wedding, Pwyll was approached by an unknown man who requested a boon. Pwyll was in such good spirits that he granted the man's request without even asking what it was—and, of course, the man turned out to Gwawl and the request he made was that he be given Rhiannon.

Rhiannon was understandably furious, but she knew Pwyll could not go back on his word—and so she formed a plan. Pwyll attended the feast celebrating the impending marriage of Rhiannon and Gwawl, but per Rhiannon's instructions, he came disguised as a beggar. He held up a small sack and asked that it be filled with food leftover from the feast. Gwawl and his men tossed food into the sack, but no matter how much they threw in, it never filled—for it was, of course, a magic sack that Rhiannon gave Pwyll for just this purpose.

Frustrated, Gwawl ordered the beggar out, but Rhiannon protested, saying they could not leave a man hungry at their wedding feast. She instructed Gwawl to stand in the sack and stomp down the food, assuring him that this would make the sack remain full. Gwawl did so, and Pwyll immediately pulled the sack up over Gwawl, cinching it tight. Pwyll and his men, who had been hiding outside, beat and kicked at Gwawl in the sack, until Gwawl called out that there was no honor in killing a man so bound. Pwyll agreed to release him, so long as Gwawl relinquished his claim on Rhiannon and any future attempts at revenge. Gwawl did so, and was never heard from again.

Rhiannon and Pwyll finally married, and eventually she bore him a son. But on the night he was born, he disappeared without a trace before he was even named. Rhiannon's maids were terrified of being put to death for having lost him, and so they decided the thing to do was to kill a puppy and smear its blood on Rhiannon's face as she lay sleeping, exhausted after childbirth.

Pwyll's court accused Rhiannon of killing and eating her own child, but despite the "evidence," Pwyll refused to believe it. Despite calls for her death, Pwyll agreed to Rhiannon's offer to do penance for the crime she did not commit. And so, in her grief and fear, she sat by the gate of the castle, telling her story to all who passed. She offered to carry them on her back, though hardly anyone accepted. And during all this, Pwyll kept her at his side as his queen, despite the anger of his court.

Meanwhile, Teyrnon, a horse lord in another part of Wales, was helping one of his mares foal when he heard a monster clawing outside the door. He rushed to see, but there was nothing but a newborn infant. He and his wife named the child Gwri Wallt Euryn, and he grew up very quickly—so quickly that, soon enough, Teyrnon recognized his resemblance to Pwyll. Teyrnon brought Gwri to Dyfed, and Rhiannon was cleared of her son's murder. She renamed him Pryderi, meaning "worry, care, loss."

—◆—

Rhiannon inspires us with her patience, fortitude, and trust. Despite so much betrayal, she remains secure within herself and her own abilities to make things right and to get what she wants. She endures and brings light.

Chapter Two
SYMBOLOGY

Symbolism in Psychology

The mind—and therefore magic—is wired to interpret our experience using symbols. At its most basic, a symbol is anything that represents something else—whether that's a concept, an object, or an action. For example, an emoji is a symbol that conveys an emotion, which is what makes it an extremely useful tool given the bland nature of texts and emails.

Symbols can be particularly useful in psychology, as they give us a framework within which we can work to understand our own emotions and experiences. If we're feeling sad, we say we feel heavyhearted, though of course our physical heart hasn't gained any weight. If we are processing a challenging life experience, we might say we feel haunted by it, or like it's something we are carrying—but again, that language is symbolic. Certainly the shadow is a symbol as well.

The way we explain emotions involves tapping into a common understanding of these symbols—and that understanding can vary from culture to culture. For instance, white flowers symbolize purity and innocence in many Western cultures, while in China they represent death and mourning. But some symbols seem to transcend culture and background, finding their way into just about every society and way of life, where they are interpreted with astounding similarity. Trickster figures can be found in all of folklore, from Rumpelstiltskin in Germany to Anansi in Ghana, from Loki in Nordic cultures to Coyote and Raven from various First Nations stories. Symbolic figures such as these are known as *archetypes*, and they can help us understand human nature. For instance, the tumultuous Greek pantheon has given us a variety of male and female archetypes, from sensuous Aphrodite to wise Athena and from authoritarian Zeus to warlike Ares. Other cultures around the world created similar archetypal gods and goddesses to symbolize certain ideals.

Carl Jung referred to this universal symbolism as the *collective unconscious*. According to Jung, it's the part of our unconscious that we received from our ancestors. This primal unconscious has been gathering and collecting our interpretations and understandings over the course of human evolution. Using mythology and folklore, Jung created a series of archetypes that can help us make meaning and share it with others. Some of these archetypes include mother, father, child, devil, wise old man, wise old woman, trickster, and hero. Regardless of where we are from or how we grew up, we have all encountered these archetypes in folklore, fiction, movies, and certainly within our own lives.

As psychology has continued to evolve since Jung, so has its understanding of the usefulness of symbolism and how best to work with it. Symbolism can allow us to talk about the specific using general terms, gaining a bit of distance from it. But symbolism is not restricted to the realm of psychology—it is also infused throughout the world of magic, and that is the region we will be exploring in this chapter.

When it comes to shadow work, symbol magic can be especially powerful, because our unconscious responds so well to symbology. Using symbols to communicate with our unconscious helps to bring what is hidden into the light, allowing it to transform.

Light a Candle for...

MARIE LAVEAU

NEW ORLEANS, 1801–1881

"Here is the day, we must welcome it with song."

—Marie Laveau

Marie Laveau was born a free Black woman in colonial New Orleans, where she worked as a healer, herbalist, and practitioner of voodoo. She was and remains known as the Voodoo Queen. She reigned for decades, mixing Catholic and African spiritual traditions in ways that people continue to practice.

She started working out of her beauty parlor, where she attended to the wealthier women of New Orleans. Her knowledge of the goings-on of New Orleans society was uncanny and garnered her the respect and even awe of the city.

In the 1830s, at the height of her popularity, Laveau held rituals in Congo Square, one of the few places in the city where free and enslaved Black people could congregate freely. She held annual ceremonies on St. John's Eve at Lake Pontchartrain, gatherings attended by thousands of people of all races. She was a religious leader and community activist, visiting prisoners and providing free lessons and rituals to those in need.

She was a living legend, and as such, it is difficult to be certain which of the stories told about her are true and which have been embellished over time. Some rumors say that she was attended at all times by a snake named Zombi, while others claim she still walks the streets of the French Quarter. She has inspired dozens of creative works, including music, books, comic series, television series, and even a musical.

Marie Laveau was buried in St. Louis Cemetery No. 1, a tiny space of only one block that still manages to hold 100,000 bodies and counting. Her mausoleum was almost immediately defaced by people who sought her power, even after her death. Many believed that if you mark her grave with three *X*'s and leave her a gift, she will grant your wish. After so many wishes, St. Louis No. 1 was closed to the public in 2015, though guided tours are available, so you can still pay homage to the Voodoo Queen.

———— ✦ ————

Marie Laveau continues to inspire to this day with her pride in her work, her creativity, and her unapologetic approach to life. She lived fully in her magic.

Symbology in Witchcraft

Symbolism has always played an incredibly influential role in witchcraft, as it has in psychology. Given the power of symbols over the mind, it makes sense that symbology is so pervasive in witchcraft. Our minds are the source of so much of our power, and symbolism is a way of focusing that power.

Archetypes

The lore of witchcraft uses a number of archetypes, just as Jung did. We can try to embody these archetypes, working to bring them into our practice, or we can call on them, invoking them to bring their energy into our spellwork.

WITCH ✦ *A witch is an archetype in and of herself. Calling someone—or calling yourself—a witch can have a couple of different meanings. Historically, it was derogatory, used to describe someone vindictive or even evil. But when the title is claimed as a positive, it can mean someone powerful, usually in a feminine, mysterious, and magical way. A witch is knowledgeable, and that knowledge comes from experience and learning from those who have come before her. She is instinctive and reactive, inventive and resourceful.*

HORNED GOD ✦ *It can be useful to think of deities as archetypes, particularly when you wish to embody their aspects, as in the creative/destructive fire of Pele or the wisdom of Odin. The Horned God is a Wiccan deity, though images of a Horned God figure date back as early as 13,000 BCE. (Remember, archetypes tend to stick around!) In Wicca, the Horned God symbolizes masculine energy, particularly regarding nature, wilderness, and sexuality. He is a dualistic god with two aspects: the Oak King and the Holly King.*

Oak King · *The Oak King represents growth and summertime; the waxing of the year. He sometimes appears as the Green Man, a figure coated entirely in oak leaves.*

Holly King · *The Holly King represents endings and wintertime; the waning of the year.*

THREEFOLD GODDESS ✦ *Triune or triple goddesses include the Charites (the three Graces), the Moirai (the three Fates), the Norns (Norse fates), Tridevi (Saraswati, Lakshmi, and Kali), and many others. They tend to represent wisdom, along with the different aspects of the life cycle and the different ways in which we embody femininity over the course of our lives. In Wicca, the Threefold Goddess has the aspects of the Maiden, the Mother, and the Crone.*

Maiden • *The Maiden represents new beginnings, birth, youth—and so she is viewed as the waxing crescent moon.*

Mother • *The Mother represents fertility, creativity, sexuality, and fulfillment— and so she is viewed as the full moon.*

Crone • *The Crone represents wisdom and endings, what we will know when we are finished—and so she is viewed as the waning crescent moon.*

How can you apply these archetypes within yourself? Are any of them in shadow? Do any of them need to be brought out into the light—embraced and embodied more fully in your life?

Symbols

We use symbols to communicate all kinds of things, from language to mathematics to road signs to hand gestures—like the thumbs-up, a peace sign, or even a middle finger. And just as there are symbols to represent certain chemical elements—like Na for sodium—there are symbols that were once used to define certain alchemical substances.

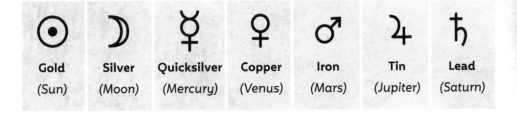

Gold	Silver	Quicksilver	Copper	Iron	Tin	Lead
(Sun)	(Moon)	(Mercury)	(Venus)	(Mars)	(Jupiter)	(Saturn)

Many witches use these same alchemical symbols, particularly when harnessing the elements or working with astrology. But there are other symbols used in magic, each of which can work as a spell if that is your intention.

Witches' marks date back to antiquity, though they were most common during the sixteenth through nineteenth centuries when ritual protection symbols known as apotropaic marks were left all over Europe and North America, often in churches and houses as well as barns and caves. The marks were usually scratched into doorways, windows, and fireplaces to safeguard all entry points.

One of the most common witch marks was a hexafoil, also known as a daisy wheel.

HEXAFOIL

The hexafoil has a variety of interpretations—it may represent the sun or a form of sacred geometry—but regardless of what it was meant to depict, it was used to cast a ritual protection spell.

Other witch marks have developed over the centuries since, with a variety of meanings that we can apply in spellwork, intention-setting, and other circumstances. The marks are a way of communicating to others that you share a common language. As we begin to explore magic and personal power and what those mean, we might feel a little fearful about sharing our magical experiences with others. Even as magic and witchcraft are being more widely and openly practiced, there is still the chance that our friends and family will judge us. Witch marks can be a kind of secret code, allowing us to invoke something private and personal, but also universal—something sacred that's also shared. After all, the word *occult* invokes the idea of "secret magic."

ÆGISHJÁLMUR

An Icelandic magical stave, or
complex rune, one of many dating
back to the seventeenth century.
Also known as the Helm of Awe, it
is meant to induce fear in battle.

ANKH

The ankh is an ancient Egyptian
hieroglyph used to represent life.
It is also known as the "key of life."
Today it is a common unisex symbol
of Black culture, embraced
by celebrities like Beyoncé
and Rihanna.

ANGURGAPI

This Icelandic stave was carved
on barrels to seal them from leaks.
Today, it could be used as
a symbol of wholeness and
impermeability.

AÐ UNNI

Another Icelandic stave,
Að unni is invoked to invite love,
usually romantic love.

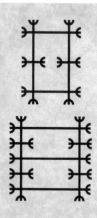

BRYNSLUSTAFIR

This Icelandic stave was carved
into whetstones, to imbue power
into the blades they sharpened.

CHAOS

From the occultist school of mystic
Aleister Crowley, this symbol of
chaos can help you break free
from constraints.

CELTIC KNOT

Also known as the triquetra, this
single intersecting line is a symbol
of three, and of infinity.

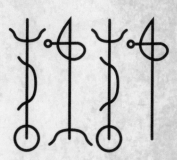

DRAUMSTAFIR

This Icelandic stave invites dreams
of desires yet to be fulfilled. It is
useful in manifestation magic.

EYE OF HORUS

Another Egyptian hieroglyph, the eye of the sky god Horus is a symbol of protection; he lost it in a battle with Set, another Egyptian deity.

HECATE'S WHEEL

The symbol of the goddess/witch Hecate is used to invoke transformation and feminine power.

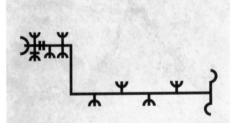

FEINGUR

An Icelandic stave to invite fertility or creativity.

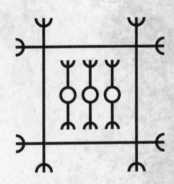

LÁSABRJÓTUR

An Icelandic stave that can help open locked doors and be used to remove the mental barriers you have inadvertently set for yourself.

MONAS HIEROGLYPHICA

This symbol was created by John Dee, Queen Elizabeth I's alchemist and astrologer. It symbolizes the sun, moon, and all the elements together.

PENTACLE

This common symbol dates all the way back to Mesopotamia. It represents the five elements (earth, air, fire, water, and soul) all bound together and can be used as a sign of protection.

OUROBOROS

This ancient Egyptian symbol of a serpent consuming its tail represents infinity and the cycle of death and rebirth.

PJÓFASTAFUR

An Icelandic stave that protects against thievery.

ROSAHRINGUR MINNI

An Icelandic stave of protection, though one that is used for everyday protection, rather than against anything major.

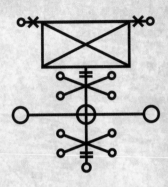

STAFFER TIL AÒ VEKJA UPP DRAUG

An Icelandic stave that can be used to invite ghosts and other spirits.

SPIRAL

The spiral is used to symbolize nature and the cycles of life.

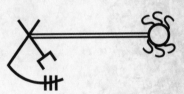

VATNAHLÍFIR

An Icelandic stave that protects against drowning.

VEGVÍSIR

An Icelandic stave that can guide you through rough waters, literal or metaphorical.

YIN AND YANG

This common symbol comes from the ancient Chinese philosophy of Taoism. It depicts the union of masculine and feminine energies, and dates back to 1000 CE.

Working with Symbol Magic

Symbol magic is fairly straightforward. Just as Icelandic fishers would carve a stave into the side of a boat to prevent drowning, you can hang a symbol of protection in your car to ward off accidents or over your doorway to bless your home. You can even wear a symbol as a necklace for protection wherever you go. Many witches have tattoos of various symbols significant to them.

But symbol magic doesn't need to be anything so permanent. Sometimes you just need the little boost of energy that a symbol can provide. Other times, you may want to keep a symbol nearby as a reminder of how to focus your energy. In that case, you might draw a symbol and sleep with it beneath your pillow for a night or two. You might tuck it into your journal or wallet as a gentle nudge. The act of drawing, holding, or wearing the symbol is the spell itself.

Sigil Magic

Sigil magic takes symbology further, allowing you to create your own symbols and assign your own meanings. It is a more personal, creative, and artistic form of symbol magic, and as such it can be even more powerful.

Sigil magic has been around for centuries and has been used by artists and magical practitioners alike. But British occultist and artist Austin Osman Spare developed a method of sigil magic that has become increasingly popular over time. Spare was a contemporary of famous English occultist Aleister Crowley, but the two of them never really saw eye to eye—Spare's approach was more about creativity and the unconscious mind and less about structure and ceremony.

Following Spare's method, you can begin by writing out an intention. For example: *I Love and Accept All That I Am*. When crafting your intention, use positive and direct phrases in the present tense—you want to be as clear and immediate as possible with your wording, as that will help the spell have a greater impact.

Next, you take the first letter of each impactful word, so *I-L-A-A-T-I-A*. Remove any repeating letters, and you have *I-L-A-T*.

Take those core letters and turn them into an artistic image. This is where you really want to allow your creativity to burst forth. You can use whatever art form you like, whether it's watercolor, collage, charcoal, calligraphy, or simply pencil and paper. Work to craft a symbol that incorporates each of the letters that remain, but also obscures them, so that they aren't entirely clear and visible to someone who doesn't already know what they are. You want to hide the meaning of your sigil, while at the same time making it a work of art.

Next, it's time to invite a little chaos magic into your sigil. As Spare describes it, the intention is to charge your creation by forgetting its precise meaning. By actively working to remove it from your conscious mind, from the light, you are moving the sigil's meaning to the unconscious and your shadow. You are making it a part of you, a part of your secret, hidden self, which will give your intention much more power to work in the world.

From there, your sigil has done all that it needs to. Like symbol magic, its existence is the spell. You can send your intention into the world by burying your sigil in the earth, casting it to the winds, dissolving it in water, or lighting it on fire. You can also keep it close by as a talisman, like you would a standard symbol.

Familiars

If you don't already know what a familiar is, think of it as a living symbol. It's a concept that cultures throughout history and around the world have embraced. Just consider terms like *spirit animal* or *'aumakua* from Indigenous traditions and how they are used to describe certain animals that have formed powerful connections with people.

Different animals symbolize different things: A lion is powerful. A lamb is innocent. A fox is clever. The animals that have been most often associated with magic tend to be "dark" animals like crows, cats, and snakes. But what makes them dark, exactly? They are animals like any other, and yet popular culture often features crows cawing, black cats bringing bad luck, and snakes as the devil in animal form. Despite, or perhaps because of, that, members of the witchy community tend to be drawn to precisely these same creatures. What is it about their perceived darkness that we relate to? Where does our connection with them lie?

Crows

Crows or their fellow corvids ravens tend to symbolize death. Since crows and ravens are carrion birds—birds who eat the carcasses of other animals—that makes sense, and yet we aren't as drawn to other carrion birds like vultures or mammals that do the same like hyenas. Crows and ravens are also extremely clever—arguably the most intelligent creatures after primates. They problem-solve, use tools, have long-term memory, and are loyal to each other. Those are qualities we all long to embody.

When you are feeling drawn to crows or when you notice them appearing in your life, they may be sending you messages in the ways that only symbols can. These messages might include:

+ *Transformation, indicating that a change is coming*

+ *Separation or loss, indicating an end of some kind*

+ *Shadow, indicating that your shadow self is calling to you*

+ *Illusion, indicating that you need to see the reality of a situation*

+ *Blocks, indicating that with ingenuity and problem-solving, you can work your way through a challenge*

Cats

A witch's familiar is most often a cat—usually a black cat. Like crows, cats are viewed as clever creatures, but also unpredictable. Anyone who has loved a cat understands that they might return your love with a purr one day and a scratch the next. Cats have strict boundaries, and that's part of what we like about them. With their rumored nine lives, they also represent death and rebirth, as well as multiple chances to get something right. Because they are nocturnal, they are associated with darkness and the shadow, with mystery and the unknown. Cats might signify:

+ *Curiosity, indicating that you should explore what you don't know with an open mind*

+ *Independence, indicating that you should trust yourself above others*

+ *Unpredictability, indicating that you should allow life to unfold without trying to force anything*

+ *Cycles, indicating the possibility of trying again and again*

Snakes

In the story of the Garden of Eden, the snake is an evil character. But there is so much more to snake mythology than what appears in the Bible, and non-Western cultures often revere these creatures as cunning and powerful figures. They are honored for their ability to shed their skins as they grow, thus transforming themselves. They also represent duality, as they symbolize both fertility—the promise of new life—and death—due to their often venomous nature. In literature, snakes are often depicted as deceptive and sexual. If you are finding yourself drawn to snakes as a symbol, that might mean:

+ *Transformation and change*

+ *Duality, or the ability to hold two contradictory facets within yourself*

+ *Sexuality or fertility*

+ *Deception, including self-deception*

Working with Familiars in Magic

A familiar can be any creature at all—they're certainly not limited to the three listed above! It can be a creature that lives with you and is close to you like a pet, but it can also be any animal you identify with. The familiars we read about in fairy tales and other folklore are a form of sympathetic magic. In this kind of magic, by working with a familiar you are able to boost your own power. But this doesn't require having actual physical access to the creature, particularly when we're working with symbolism.

More often, familiar magic involves choosing to form an intentional connection with a certain creature that has meaning for you. That meaning can be rooted in folklore of a specific culture or it can come from your own personal experience. As with other symbol magic, the creature itself is the spell. The connection you form with your familiar creates the magic.

CREATIVITY SPELL

Sometimes it can be useful to harness symbols that come from a tradition that precedes modern times, rather than creating your own—particularly if you aren't feeling all that creative! When you need a little inspiration boost, consider embodying an archetype. Do you want to think of yourself as a witch with all the attendant mystery and power? Or do you want to manifest as the Horned God, replete with wildness and passion? Or would you like to see yourself as a form of the Threefold Goddess?

There are many ways to do this, and the simplest and often most powerful is simply *deciding* to. Just as we pick which clothes to wear every day, we can choose which archetype we want to embody. If you would like, you can take that further and dress a little "witchier," wilder, or whatever else makes you *feel* more like that archetype— because whatever makes you feel a certain way can influence you to actually *become* that way. You can also use an essential oil that sparks whatever feeling you're going for, since scent is one of the most potent ways to stimulate the unconscious. Perhaps a pine essential oil will make you feel more like the Oak King. Try a patchouli essential oil to feel more like the Mother.

Your choice to embody an archetype is the spell. You can add power to it by incorporating a magical symbol, one that has soaked up centuries' worth of intention and enchantment from magical practitioners of the past. What symbol speaks to the kind of creativity you want to invite today? Is it the alchemical symbol for fire? Is it feingur, or the symbol of chaos? You might draw that symbol on your palm—using nontoxic ink, of course—sketch it into your daily journal, or carry it around with you on a slip of paper. Its power will flow with you, bringing more creativity to your day.

INTUITION SPELL

Sigil magic is ideal for working to bring forth your intuition, as it is designed to push your conscious mind out of the way and allow what lies in the shadow to come to the surface.

Begin by selecting a phrase that captures your intention. Be as specific as possible, so rather than writing something like *I Would Like to Be More Intuitive*, consider going deeper. If you are looking to explore a new career, you might write something like *My Intuition Will Guide Me Toward a Career That Will Provide Me with Freedom, Creativity, Joy, and Prosperity.*

Once you have your phrase, take your time crafting your sigil. Turn back to page 41 for a reminder on how it works. There is no reason to rush this—instead, find joy in the process. Don't think too hard about how to incorporate the letters, just let your creativity—and yes, your intuition!—flow. Make your sigil into a work of art.

When you've finished, meditate with your sigil. As you gaze upon it, work to call forth your shadow. This is the part of you that responds best to sigil magic—to intuition, creativity, and flow. As often happens when we summon our shadow, you may feel emotions come to the surface as well as thoughts and memories you might typically try to avoid. Let them in. Allow them to be a part of your experience, and use them to give power to your sigil.

And then, let your sigil go. Consider how you want to do this based on which element will best serve you and your intention:

✦

AIR will invite new energy, life, and movement.
Tear your sigil into small pieces and let them scatter in the wind.

✦

EARTH will ground you, helping you feel safe and secure.
Bury your sigil in the earth.

✦

FIRE will create and destroy, allowing for new beginnings.
Set your sigil aflame.

✦

WATER will bring you clarity and awareness.
Dissolve your sigil in clear water.

SELF-LOVE SPELL

There are a couple of different ways to work with familiars in self-love spells, depending on what you need. If you're feeling like you just want to bask in a little warmth and affection, you might treat yourself by spending time with a familiar that gives you those sensations. Maybe that means spending time with your pet, or if you don't have a pet, visiting your local shelter to exchange some love with an animal in need. It might be as simple as watching funny cat videos on YouTube.

But it can also mean working with these familiars as you would an archetype. How about allowing yourself to be bumbling and silly like a kitten? Or bursting with affection and loyalty like a dog? Looking for these qualities in yourself can be a powerful act of self-love.

Alternatively, your shadow might be at work in you, and you may be feeling like you can't find any positive qualities in yourself. We all get that way sometimes. And in times like those it can be helpful to choose a familiar that perhaps isn't quite so universally beloved.

Consider a creature that you don't normally have affection for like a spider or a worm.

Maybe, at first, it doesn't feel that good to compare yourself to one of these creatures, which also happen to thrive in dark places. But if you sit and think about it, you can find all manner of positive qualities in each of them. Spiders protect us from other, more harmful, invaders, and they inspire us with their ingenuity, their artistry, and their perseverance. Worms are agents of transformation, working unseen to renew the soil and provide the earth with sustenance. These same qualities can be found within you. What else can you realize about yourself and what you have to offer? What else can you love about yourself?

Light a Candle for...

BABA YĀGA

SLAVIC FOLKLORE, ~UNKNOWN

The obedient children arrived at the forest and, oh, wonder! there stood a hut, and what a curious one! It stood on tiny hen's feet, and at the top was a rooster's head.
—Folk Tales from the Russian, by Verra Xenophontovna Kalamatiano de Blumenthal

Baba Yaga features in so many tales of Slavic folklore, including stories being written today. She lives in a hut with chicken legs that can pick up and move and flies around in a mortar and pestle. She's typically pictured as a sly old woman with bony legs, a long, crooked nose, piercing eyes, and iron teeth, but unlike Hansel & Gretel's witch or other fairytale witches, she's not necessarily evil.

When she is encountered in the woods by Ivan Tsarevich, Vasilisa the Beautiful, or other Slavic folkloric heroes, she often aids them in their quests, albeit in a fairly threatening way. Baba Yaga might grant wishes, but she might just as easily pop you in her oven and eat you. If she does provide assistance, it is only after you have earned her respect by completing her assigned tasks . . . and if you don't, the odds of being eaten definitely go up.

In legends, Baba Yaga is considered a contradictory character—one who is frightening, but not necessarily evil. She is always treated with respect and can see into the heart of anyone she encounters. She knows whether or not someone is worthy and rewards the virtuous with knowledge. In the story of Vasilisa the Beautiful, Baba Yaga acted as both the villain and the wisewoman, setting the already beleaguered Vasilisa to impossible housecleaning tasks. (Vasilisa was a Cinderella figure with an abusive stepmother.) But when Vasilisa, with the help of her magic doll, completed the tasks, Baba Yaga gave her the power to free herself from her stepmother, and Vasilisa eventually went on to marry the czar.

Baba Yaga is said to have control over the weather and the elements, and her powers are always associated with the wilderness and femininity—storms, forests, kitchen work, and so forth. She is unpredictable and tempestuous, but ultimately a positive force of nature.

———◆———

Baba Yaga takes some of the so-called negative aspects of femininity—emotion, unpredictability—and makes them powerful aspects that demand respect. Her magic is intuitive and wild, and she lives by her own rules, making her own choices.

Chapter Three
THE UNSEEN

We explore the Unseen through divination, and when working with shadow magic, this process is focused within, rather than without. Some magical practitioners can work to see the future or to read someone else's mind, but shadow magic is about uncovering what is already there within us but hidden. And honestly, nothing is more difficult to see than those things we have concealed from ourselves.

Our shadow is the source of our intuition—the knowledge we have that we cannot explain with logic or reason. Making the effort to bring forth and interpret our intuition is, therefore, our act of divination.

Divination will never tell you anything you don't already know. It is merely a way to tap into your deep internal knowing as you invite yourself to answer your own question. You may not always like the response you get—we often refuse to accept things even when we know them to be true—but it is *your* answer nevertheless.

There are many tools we can use in divination and many paths that can light our way. Some will work better for you than others, and it can be useful to experiment with and practice several different forms of divination to determine what best sparks your intuition, creativity, and sense of connection. Let's look at a few options you can explore.

Tasseomancy

Tasseomancy is the practice of reading tea leaves. It's fairly straightforward in execution: You brew a cup of tea using loose leaves and no strainer so that the dried leaves are floating around in the water. As you drink your tea, hold the cup in your hands and focus on the question you want your intuition to answer. When you've finished your tea and there is just a bit of liquid and leaves left at the bottom, swirl what remains three times—or any number of times that has significant meaning for you—in a counterclockwise direction and then upend the cup onto a saucer or other small plate. Once it's had a moment to drain, flip the cup back right side up, and take a look at the images you can find in the shapes of the tea leaves left in the cup and on the saucer.

Tasseomancy definitely requires using a lot of imagination and creativity. If you don't *want* to see symbols in your tea, you won't. But if you are open to the possibilities, they will reveal themselves. Remember, you are trying to help your shadow speak, to help your intuition come forth. If it feels like you're making stuff up, guess what—you are! That's how creativity works. You'll probably see multiple shapes and images in both the cup and the saucer, and it's your task to determine how they relate to each other and how they relate to you. This is *your* reading, so you make the rules.

As you attempt to interpret the shapes you see, it can be useful to turn to traditional symbology. Tasseomancy has been around for thousands of years, and the symbols for interpreting the leaves have also been passed down. This is just a small sampling of the possibilities:

Apple ✦ *Wisdom, or often love or friendship*

Bird ✦ *Change is coming, or a journey*

Dagger ✦ *Challenges lie ahead*

Dog ✦ *Loyalty, protection*

Fish ✦ *Emotion, creativity*

Flower ✦ *Beauty, love*

Four-Leaf Clover ✦ *Luck*

Hourglass ✦ *Focus on the present moment*

Sun ✦ *New beginnings, energy*

Tree ✦ *Strength, certainty*

Wand ✦ *Creativity, power*

You might find that these meanings don't hold much power for you. After all, you may have personal associations with these symbols that don't match their universal meanings. In that case, you should absolutely go with your own interpretation, trusting your instincts and intuition. That's what divination is all about.

Cartomancy

One of the most common forms of divination is cartomancy, or the use of cards. These can be oracle cards, which are cards with evocative images that you can use to interpret your own experience. The most common oracle deck is a tarot deck, simply because this is a system that has been in use for so very long.

Tarot started off as a parlor game, used in the same way we use playing cards today. But there was often a lot more artistry involved. The Visconti-Sforza, the oldest known tarot deck, dates back to the fifteenth century, and it was hand-painted and intricate, featuring figures that are archetypes of tarot today.

In the eighteenth century, people began turning to tarot for divination. Jean-Baptiste Alliette, a French occultist who went by the name of Etteilla, created and published a revamped tarot deck that assigned a specific meaning to each of the cards. He incorporated ideas about astronomy, as well as the elements of fire, air, water, and earth, and set about using the symbolism derived from all of these to create archetypes for each of the cards. These archetypes could be used to understand and interpret our experience (i.e., divination).

In 1909, the writer A. E. Waite worked with the artist Pamela Colman Smith to create another deck. Today, that deck is known as the Rider-Waite-Smith deck (with Rider being the publisher), and it is considered a classic in the tarot canon. Smith and Waite were both members of a secret society, known as the Hermetic Order of the Golden Dawn, devoted to the study of the occult. (Other members included Aleister Crowley and W. B. Yeats.) This deck was much easier to use, with archetypes that were more readily understood and applicable to daily life—and more open to interpretation, allowing us to use our intuition to explain the cards, rather than puzzling over a meaning that doesn't make sense or doesn't feel true to our lives.

The illustrations in the Rider-Waite-Smith deck tell an intricate story when they are laid out, a kind of hero's journey through darkness and back out into the light. But some of the archetypes they used don't have quite as much resonance today as they did a hundred years ago. (When was the last time you encountered a hierophant or a hermit? Or a knight, for that matter?) So the assigned meanings have evolved over the years to reflect our modern experience, though the names of the cards have remained the same.

Today, you can purchase tarot decks featuring vintage cartoons, Disney villains, cats of all kinds, and Dungeons & Dragons, just to name a few recent iterations. This proliferation of tarot decks is fantastic, because it means there are more options to choose from. The idea behind picking a deck is to find one that speaks to *you*—that your shadow and your intuition can recognize and communicate with.

As with all forms of divination, tarot is always accurate . . . because all it's doing is revealing what you already know to be true deep down. Tarot can help you see the truth of what you know instinctively but haven't yet accepted consciously. As with all shadow work, that can mean either confronting some hard truths or discovering some dreamy possibilities that have so far seemed *impossible*. Laying out tarot cards allows you to lay down and explore your own hidden truths.

The Cards

There are two parts to a tarot deck: the Major Arcana and the Minor Arcana. The Major Arcana consists of the first twenty-two cards in the deck, and they are sometimes said to be more important, but that isn't necessarily true. They do cover some big concepts—like change and love and duality—but all tarot cards have meaning and their meaning is determined by *you*. As with all symbolism, an archetype only means what it means to you. The Minor Arcana includes four suits, much like an ordinary deck of cards, each with its own meanings.

The Major Arcana

0. THE FOOL

The wisdom and innocence of childhood, and the possibilities of growth

1. THE MAGICIAN

Skill and capability, hard work and achievement

2. THE HIGH PRIESTESS

The feminine aspect of the Magician. Equally powerful, but with more mysticism, mystery, and intuition

3. THE EMPRESS

Nurturing and sensuous, embracing creativity and fertility

4. THE EMPEROR

Justice and fairness, within the structure of tradition

5. THE HIEROPHANT

Established belief systems, including religion, society, and politics

6. THE LOVERS

Relationships, of the romantic sort or between two disparate parts of yourself

7. THE CHARIOT

The work that goes into finding a balance between oppositional parts

8. STRENGTH

The ability to get through a difficulty

9. THE HERMIT

Time spent in contemplation, alone and away from outside influence

10. WHEEL OF FORTUNE

A force for good, guiding you through life's ups and downs

11. JUSTICE

Fairness, truth, and karma

12. THE HANGED MAN

The sacrifices we make in pursuit of knowledge, self-awareness, and truth

13. DEATH

An ending, a change—as in the death of a way of approaching the world

14. TEMPERANCE

Slow and measured contemplation, and openness to advice from others

15. THE DEVIL

Self-deception or self-sabotage

16. THE TOWER

A painful change that might require starting over

17. THE STAR

New beginnings, renewal

18. THE MOON

Illusions, unconscious fears, the shadow

19. THE SUN

Clarity, confidence, and positivity

20. JUDGMENT

Evaluation of past choices and different choices that can be made in the future

21. THE WORLD

Hard work soon to be paid off

The Minor Arcana

The four suits of the Minor Arcana include Cups, Pentacles, Swords, and Wands, each of which governs a specific part of daily life.

CUPS

The suit of Cups manages the relationships we have with those around us, including our families, friends, coworkers, neighbors, and more. This suit is dominated by emotion, so choices made under the guidance of Cups are made from the heart, rather than the mind.

ACE OF CUPS

A new relationship

TWO OF CUPS

Unity, attraction, and intimacy

THREE OF CUPS

A celebration of friendship
and cooperation

FOUR OF CUPS

Loneliness, apathy,
self-absorption

FIVE OF CUPS

Regret and grief

SIX OF CUPS

Nostalgia for what has been lost

SEVEN OF CUPS

A chance to begin again

EIGHT OF CUPS

Dissatisfaction and disappointment

NINE OF CUPS

Bliss and fulfillment

TEN OF CUPS

Happy, healthy relationships

PAGE OF CUPS

Potential, childlike curiosity,
possibility

KNIGHT OF CUPS

Romance, but with a
dose of fantasy

QUEEN OF CUPS

Nurturing and intuitive

KING OF CUPS

The balance of logic and emotion

PENTACLES

A practical suit, Pentacles govern the work of meeting your basic needs and goals—including financial and professional success.

ACE OF PENTACLES
Potential for financial abundance

TWO OF PENTACLES
The ability to work efficiently

THREE OF PENTACLES
Collaboration and organization

FOUR OF PENTACLES
The halting of progress

FIVE OF PENTACLES
Isolation, worry, monetary concerns

SIX OF PENTACLES
Generosity from others

SEVEN OF PENTACLES
Assessment: Do you continue on your path or start anew?

EIGHT OF PENTACLES
Hard work and dedication

NINE OF PENTACLES
Success and self-sufficiency

TEN OF PENTACLES
Long-term wealth and stability

PAGE OF PENTACLES
Capability, learning new skills

KNIGHT OF PENTACLES
Productivity, hard work, focus

QUEEN OF PENTACLES
Nurturing yet practical, like a working mom

KING OF PENTACLES
Confident leader, like a CEO

SWORDS

The suit of Swords is the suit of conflict—the struggles we have with others and the struggles we have within ourselves. Swords are ruled by logic and by provable fact.

ACE OF SWORDS
A breakthrough of new ideas

TWO OF SWORDS
A difficult decision

THREE OF SWORDS
Pain and heartbreak

FOUR OF SWORDS
Rest and recovery

FIVE OF SWORDS
Defeat and resentment

SIX OF SWORDS
Letting go, choosing a new outlook

SEVEN OF SWORDS
Strategy, manipulation

EIGHT OF SWORDS
Self-doubt, limiting beliefs

NINE OF SWORDS
Anxiety, fear, depression

TEN OF SWORDS
A crisis or ordeal

PAGE OF SWORDS
Seek out new knowledge and perspective

KNIGHT OF SWORDS
Ambition, impulsivity

QUEEN OF SWORDS
Boundaries, hard truths

KING OF SWORDS
Advice, intellectual authority

WANDS

Wands are the suit of creativity, passion, and energy. There is inspiration and desire when these cards are drawn.

ACE OF WANDS

Enthusiasm, creativity

TWO OF WANDS

Planning, goal-setting

THREE OF WANDS

Progress, sharing of ideas

FOUR OF WANDS

Early successes

FIVE OF WANDS

Roadblocks, conflicting opinions

SIX OF WANDS

Success, self-confidence

SEVEN OF WANDS

Competition, perseverance

EIGHT OF WANDS

Action, leaping forward

NINE OF WANDS

Resilience, strength, capability

TEN OF WANDS

Completion, responsibility, commitment

PAGE OF WANDS

Freedom, curiosity, flow

KNIGHT OF WANDS

Energy, passion, impulsivity

QUEEN OF WANDS

Determination, power, courage

KING OF WANDS

Vision, big picture, dedication

How to Do a Reading

The most important thing to remember when doing a tarot reading is that *you* are in charge of the reading. The cards will mean what they mean to you, and the meanings given above aren't rules, merely guidelines. You can do a reading by pulling just one card, or even by laying out an entire deck—though that's not really recommended, as it can get extremely confusing.

That said, it can be helpful to give yourself a little structure as you get used to working with your cards. Begin by shuffling your cards and asking them a question—remembering, of course, that the person answering that question will be you. Next, pick a spread that will be most helpful in answering that question. There are many different spreads to choose from, and the more complex the spread, the more complex your answer will be.

THREE-CARD SPREAD

This simple spread can be used to answer most everyday questions, and you can always lay another card down if you require a little more clarity. Once you've shuffled, fan the cards out facedown in an arc, so that the back of each card is available to you. And then consider how to choose your three cards. Look for one that is poking out or for one that is hidden. You can wave your hands over the cards, feeling for warmth or energy. Let your intuition be your guide.

Then lay each card down from left to right.

FIRST CARD: Left	**SECOND CARD: Center**	**THIRD CARD: Right**
Choose whether this represents the past, your conscious self, or whatever else is most useful for you.	*Choose whether this represents the present, your shadow self, or whatever else is most useful for you.*	*Choose whether this represents the future, what is most alive for you today, or whatever else is most useful for you.*

GUIDANCE SPREAD

This more complex spread can be very useful in determining the answers to complicated questions, like what you really want and what you should do, particularly when you're having trouble seeing all sides of an issue. With this spread, you'll draw eight cards, placing the first card off to one side, and the remaining seven cards all in a row together.

FIRST CARD
Your primary concern, the issue at hand

SECOND CARD	THIRD CARD	FOURTH CARD	FIFTH CARD
What is motivating you to seek guidance?	*The area(s) in your life that are causing anxiety*	*Elements in your situation you may not be consciously aware of*	*Information that will help you overcome your apprehensions*

SIXTH CARD	SEVENTH CARD	EIGHTH CARD
Help in letting your anxieties go	*Advice on how to move forward*	*How it may all work out, if you follow the path*

Lithomancy

Lithomancy is the art of reading stones, most often Nordic runes. This practice can be expanded to include osteomancy (see page 71), which is the reading of cast bones, usually animal bones, and the reading of ritual sticks, including the Celtic Ogham, a medieval alphabet. Feel free to explore materials to find the one that unlocks your own shadow best.

To perform lithomancy, all you need are the stones or sticks themselves and a casting mat, which can be as simple as a plain cloth. You can pull a few runes or bones, as you would tarot cards, or for a more complex reading, you can toss the whole set onto the mat, reading the ones that fall on the mat from left to right. See how they relate to one another, using your intuition and your shadow self to interpret them.

Nordic Runes

The Elder Futhark, a set of Nordic runes, dates back to the second century and is believed to have been used for divination as well as communication. The word *rune* in fact translates to "secret." But because these runes were so mysterious, there isn't much historical evidence for how they were used or by whom. The only traces we have, really, are in the oral histories that were passed down over generations, and as we all know, facts tend to shift when stories are being told and retold.

So the truth is we don't actually know the precise meanings behind each of these runes—which is actually very useful for you as a rune-reader. You can use these meanings as a jumping-off point, but as with tasseomancy, cartomancy, and other forms of divination, the true meanings are best found within yourself.

FEHU ✦ CATTLE
A rune of abundance, luck, and energy, representing new beginnings

URUZ ✦ AUROCHS (WILD OX)
A rune of determination, stubbornness, and pushing boundaries. Can also be used for healing.

THURISAZ ✦ GIANT, THORNS
A rune of protection

ANSUZ ✦ DIVINE BREATH
A rune of order, stability, and communication

RAIDHO ✦ JOURNEY

*A rune of exploration,
preparation, and forethought*

KENAZ ✦ TORCH

*A rune of knowledge
and inspiration*

GEBO ✦ GIFT

*A rune of the Golden Rule—
giving unto others, and receiving
in return; community*

WUNJO ✦ JOY

*A rune of desire, romantic love, as
well as contentment and harmony.
Can dispel pain and suffering.*

HAGALAZ ✦ HAIL

*A rune of crisis, signifying
a coming change*

NAUTHIZ ✦ NECESSITY

*A rune of work,
strength, and willpower*

ISA ✦ ICE

*A rune of stillness and
concentration. Can also
represent stagnation.*

JERA ✦ HARVEST

*A rune of the cycle of life, in all
its ups and downs*

EIHWAZ ✦ YEW TREE

*A rune of birth and death,
symbolizing new beginnings.
Can be used for protection.*

PERTHRO ✦ FATE

*A rune of secrets and the unknown—
which cannot be seen but can still
influence us*

ALGIZ ✦ ELK

A rune that invites your intuition. Can also be used for protection.

SOWILO ✦ SUN

A rune of strength, confidence, and a sense of wholeness

TIWAZ ✦ CREATOR

A rune of sacrifice, greater good, and giving to others

BERKANO ✦ BIRCH TREE

A rune of feminine power or creativity, insight, healing, and nurturing

EHWAZ ✦ HORSE

A rune of freedom, motion, and independence, but also cooperation

MANNAZ ✦ HUMANKIND

A rune of community, responsibility to others, and the joys of living in harmony. Also a rune of intelligence.

LAGUZ ✦ WATER

A rune of life, dreams, mystery, imagination, and emotion

INGUZ ✦ SEED

A rune of creativity and fertility surrounding internal work. About creating a force within yourself before sharing it with others.

DAGAZ ✦ DAWN

A rune of balance between light and dark

OTHALA ✦ HOUSEHOLD

A rune of home and hearth, as well as family, including ancestors

Osteomancy

The history of bone divination has existed for thousands of years, all around the world, including in places as varied as Japan, Korea, North Africa, the Middle East, areas of Europe with Germanic and Celtic roots, Serbia, and Greece. During the Shang dynasty in China, around 1500 BCE, a common practice called pyro-osteomancy involved burning an ox's shoulder blade and then examining the cracks that developed in it. The most common form of osteomancy referenced today derives from American hoodoo traditions, which were brought over by enslaved peoples from Africa. If you are considering practicing osteomancy, it's important to approach it with a spirit of inquiry and respect, to avoid cultural appropriation and honor the traditions from which it originated.

Working with bones is simply another way to work with nature—after all, death is a part of our existence, and the more we shy away from it, the more fear we feel. Osteomancy can be particularly useful for shadow magic, when you are exploring the darkest parts of yourself, including your greatest fears.

But sourcing those bones can be surprisingly challenging! You don't want to just use the carcass from last night's roast chicken, nor is it advisable to go digging around in roadkill. Instead, you can purchase bones from online stores that have properly cleaned them and sourced them ethically. You can also use shells, which are the bones of the sea; bark or sticks, which are the bones of trees; or even rocks, which we can think of as the bones of the earth.

Before you begin, you can etch them with certain markings to make it easier to tell them apart. Then it is up to you to choose how many bones you want to use and to assign them meanings. You might consider choosing a bone for each area of your internal and external life, including:

+ Family
+ Friends
+ Home
+ Career
+ Abundance
+ Self-care
+ Love
+ Challenges
+ Creativity
+ Fears
+ Dreams

Light a Candle for...

MOTHER SHIPTON

YORKSHIRE, 1488–1561

"When the cow doth ride the bull, then, priest, beware the skull."
—Mother Shipton's Prophecies

Ursula Southeil, also known as Mother Shipton, was a legendary prophetess born in a cave in North Yorkshire. Contemporary descriptions of Mother Shipton call her "hunched" with a large, crooked nose, making Mother Shipton the archetypal witch and the inspiration for everything from Disney witches to Halloween costumes in Target.

She was born in a cave and lived in the woods with her mother until she was two years old. That cave is known today as Mother Shipton's Cave. At the time, it was said that the skull-shaped pool of water inside the cave was capable of turning objects to stone, though now we know those objects are just stalagmites. Ursula's mother taught her the ways of herb magic, which she continued to study into adulthood.

Despite the townsfolk's fear of her, she became a valuable hedge witch—so much so that she was eventually accepted into the community, and even married a local carpenter named Toby Shipton. A month after her marriage, a neighbor came to her for help, saying that someone had stolen her new smock and petticoat. Mother Shipton told her not to worry, they would get the items back the next day—and indeed, at market the next morning, the woman who had stolen the clothes was wearing them over her own and dancing around the square, singing "I stole my Neighbor's Smock and Coat, I am a Thief, and here I show't." Afterward she handed Mother Shipton the smock and petticoat, curtsied, and departed.

This is just one of dozens of stories of Mother Shipton's prowess, and her fame only grew when, after her husband died, she returned to living in her cave. Visitors would travel vast distances to solicit her help and receive potions and spells. She began making prophecies, and they would come true. A bridge that she claimed would collapse did. She predicted the marriage of Henry VIII to Anne Boleyn and rightly foretold that it would lead to the downfall of the Catholic Church in England. Her prophecies were collected into books, and the first known edition was published eighty years after her death.

——◆——

Our O.G. witch, Mother Shipton, transformed her numerous challenges—physical disabilities, impoverishment, illegitimate birth—into virtues and rightfully convinced those who would deprive her of her power and value.

Ogham

Ogham is an early medieval Celtic alphabet. It can be found inscribed into various stone pillars across Ireland and Wales and is thought to have been a form of cryptography—a way of leaving secret messages that couldn't be interpreted by invading Romans. As with the Elder Futhark, we don't know all that much about Ogham and how it was used. There is mention of using Ogham for divination in Tochmarc Etaíne, an early Irish mythological text; in it, the druid Dylan takes four wands made of yew and inscribes them with Ogham letters, using them to divine a path. How exactly he does this isn't stated, so as with all other forms of divination, it's up to you and your intuition to figure out how to work with Ogham.

Most often, Ogham is cast upon a cloth in much the same way we cast runes or bones. The meanings of each symbol in the Ogham alphabet are very much open to interpretation. The ones listed below are based in folklore and divination practices that have been passed down over the years. Traditionally, Ogham is carved onto five sticks, with the alphabet growing upward like a tree.

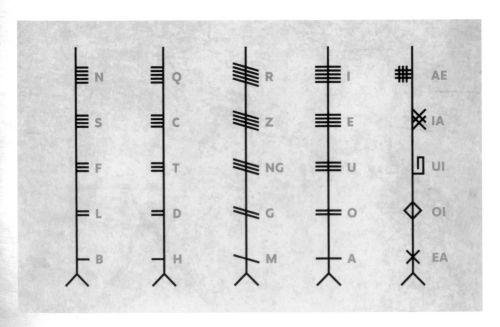

B, Beith ✦ *The birch tree, representative of new beginnings, change, and purification*

L, Luis ✦ *The rowan tree, representative of insight, protection, and blessings*

F, Fearn ✦ *The alder tree, representative of the connection between the seen and unseen worlds*

S, Saille ✦ *The willow tree, representative of knowledge and spiritual growth*

N, Nion ✦ *The ash tree, representative of the connection between the inner and outer self, and of creativity*

H, Huath ✦ *The hawthorn tree, representative of cleansing, protection, and defense*

D, Duir ✦ *The oak tree, representative of strength, resilience, and self-confidence*

T, Tinne ✦ *The holly tree, representative of immortality, courage, and protection*

C, Coll ✦ *The hazel tree, representative of life, wisdom, creativity, and knowledge*

Q, Quert ✦ *The apple tree, representative of love, faith, and rebirth*

M, Muin ✦ *The grapevine, representative of prophecy and truth*

G, Got ✦ *The ivy, representative of growth, wildness, and the cycle of rebirth*

Ng, nGeatal ✦ *The reed, representative of health, healing, and community*

Z/St, Straith ✦ *The blackthorn tree, representative of authority, strength, and control*

R, Ruis ✦ *The elder tree, representative of endings, maturity, and wisdom*

A, Ailim ✦ *The elm tree, representative of flexibility, clarity of vision, and long-term goals*

O, Onn ✦ *The gorse, representative of long-term plans, determination, and perseverance*

U, Uhr ✦ *The heather, representative of passion, generosity, and healing*

E, Eadhadh ✦ *The aspen, representative of endurance, courage, and success*

I, Iodhadh ✦ *The yew, representative of endings, rebirth, and change*

Ea, Eabhadh ✦ *The grove, representative of multiple trees, symbolizing connection, conflict resolution, and justice*

Oi, Our ✦ *The spindle tree, representative of strength, hard work, and family*

Ui, Uillean ✦ *The honeysuckle, representative of strong will, desires, and dreams*

Ia, Ifin ✦ *The pine, representative of clarity of vision and the release of guilt*

Ae, Amhancholl ✦ *The witch hazel, representative of purity, cleansing, and new beginnings*

Pendulum Divination

Sometimes you just need a quick answer, and in that case, a pendulum can be an incredibly useful tool. You can use anything as a pendulum, whether it's a necklace with a charm on it or a piece of rock tied to a string—all that's required is a little weight and free movement. Some witches like to keep a specific pendulum on hand just for the purpose of divination—this can imbue the pendulum with your energy and intention, giving it more focus and power.

When choosing a pendulum, consider what kind of metal you want the chain to be made of and what kind of stone or crystal you want. Different metals have different meanings, and the same goes for crystals. Again, the most important meaning is the one that is personal to you, so check in with your emotional and intuitive response to the pendulum as you select it. This is by no means a complete list of metals and crystals and their meanings, but these are the ones most commonly used for pendulums. (Though again, you can use anything you like!)

Metals

Gold ✦ *The sun and energy*

Stainless Steel ✦ *Strength and power*

Sterling Silver ✦ *The moon and mystery*

Crystals

Amethyst ✦ *Intuition and meditation*

Aquamarine ✦ *Personal truth*

Bloodstone ✦ *Courage and vitality*

Calcite ✦ *Amplification of energy*

Clear Quartz ✦ *Healing and channeling*

Fluorite ✦ *Decision-making*

Garnet ✦ *Creativity*

Hematite ✦ *Protection and grounding*

Labradorite ✦ *Seeing past blocks and illusions*

Lapis Lazuli ✦ *Focus and amplification*

Moonstone ✦ *Peace and harmony*

Obsidian ✦ *Protection and facing fears*

Opal ✦ *Mystical power and creativity*

Rose Quartz ✦ *Love, in all its forms*

Selenite ✦ *Purification*

Smoky Quartz ✦ *Protection and fertility*

Sunstone ✦ *Energy and creativity*

Tigereye ✦ *Personal power and integrity*

As with all crystals, it's important to cleanse your pendulum before you use it and to repeat the cleansing process regularly. Depending on the properties of the crystal, you can do this by soaking it in hot water or by allowing it to rest in moonlight or sunlight for several hours.

Next, you'll want to familiarize yourself with your pendulum and allow your pendulum to become familiar with you. Hold the end of the chain in your dominant hand, suspending the stone. Begin by asking it straightforward questions that you already consciously know the answers to. (Again, you already know the answers to *all* the questions you might ask your pendulum, but you may not know them consciously!)

Watch your pendulum to see how it answers. Does it swing back and forth for no, and side to side for yes? Or vice versa? Does it spin in a circle? Which direction means yes, and which direction means no? Continue asking your pendulum questions until communication between the two of you grows clear.

Once you've established the language you and your pendulum will share, it becomes very easy to quickly get the answers you are looking for. All you'll need to do is find a space, both mentally and physically, where you can clear your mind, allowing your shadow to come forth. Ask the question, aloud or silently—whatever feels best to you—and let the answer come.

Pyschography

Automatic writing, also known as psychography, is the practice of writing without awareness, allowing your shadow to spill out of you and onto the page. This practice can unleash a special magic within, giving you the ability to uncover whatever you may have been hiding from yourself.

This practice can seem a little intimidating. Often we hide things from ourselves because we find them too painful to look at. What if what comes spilling out is a stream of vitriol and suffering?

If that's the case—then so be it. Remember, your sadness and fears make up only part of your shadow and are not synonymous with it. It's important to note, though, that psychography doesn't necessarily produce a sludge of despair—in fact, it hardly ever does! More often than not, psychography will reveal a forgotten memory, a secret dream or ambition, a different perspective on the world or a situation, or just an odd, quirky thought that illuminates a facet of yourself, of your creativity and uniqueness, that you never really considered or appreciated before. These are also parts of your shadow that can be brought forth through writing.

All in all, psychography is simply another way of getting to know yourself better, to integrate your shadow in all of its facets.

How to Practice Psychography

At its core, psychography is a lot like freewriting, where you simply put down whatever comes to mind without worrying about punctuation or sentence structure or anything like that. But it can sometimes be difficult for our conscious awareness to get out of the way. We still find ourselves *thinking* about what to write, rather than simply allowing the words to flow.

There are some ways to offset this tendency, and they involve reaching into your mystical tool kit and applying those same strategies to this new practice. Start by creating a ritual out of your psychography magic. Set aside a time and place, and do some relaxation practices to calm the conscious mind, like meditation, breathwork, or yoga.

Then set yourself up in a space that feels good and right. You might use some essential oils that are supportive of this kind of exploration, like sage, lavender, or frankincense. You could dab them on the soles of your feet or use a diffuser. You might also keep some crystals nearby, like lapis lazuli, opal, malachite, or amethyst. You might play some music that soothes and inspires you. It can also be helpful to use a journal and pen or pencil set aside for exactly this purpose.

And then . . . simply be. Allow whatever wants to come out of you to do so, and try not to force anything. This definitely takes practice, but it gets easier as you get used to the sensation of releasing, rather than pulling, the words from within you. It may be helpful to ask a specific question of yourself . . . or it might not. It depends on what you're looking for.

Write for as long as feels right. When you're finished, you're finished, whether it's pages and pages, or just a sentence or two.

When you're done, set down your pen and close your eyes. Let that flow you've released within yourself settle, pooling inside you like a calm pond rather than a river.

When you feel ready, read back over what you wrote. Underline or circle the phrases or words that feel particularly true, and draw inspiration, meaning, or release where you can.

Psychography is just a tool to allow you to access the information you carry within, whether it's your fears or your dreams. Only you can truly interpret it.

Scrying

Scrying is the art of peering into an element, usually fire or water, to try to divine what might be hidden. You can look into a bowl of water, a candle, a mirror—which, in feng shui, is a representation of the element of water—or even a crystal ball.

If there are some loose guidelines involved in tasseomancy, cartomancy, and the other forms of divination, there are almost *no* guidelines when it comes to scrying. It is an art that is guided entirely by *you,* by what speaks to you and what you speak to it.

To get into the proper frame of mind for scrying, you'll want to reach a meditative state much like the one used in psychography. You can set yourself up for this in a similar way—by creating an environment conducive to magic, particularly internal magic. Start by choosing your medium for scrying. What are you looking to see?

CANDLE ✦ A candle or other form of fire can be helpful if you are looking to create or spark something. It can also serve you well if you are feeling low or out of sorts, acting as a literal light in the darkness. Alternatively, if there's something you want to let go of, the destructive power of fire can help you release whatever has been unconsciously holding you back.

WATER ✦ A bowl of water is a peaceful, gentle medium for scrying. It is reflective, but also naturally distorted, so that you can peer into it without getting caught up in what is "real" or not. Scrying into water can be a way of swimming toward your innermost self, diving deep and finding the resources and clarity you hold within.

MIRROR ✦ Mirror scrying can be a little tricky, as it's easy to get caught up in looking at our perceived flaws. But it can also be incredibly powerful, particularly for self-love magic.

CRYSTAL BALL ✦ *A crystal ball can be the most powerful of all, simply because of all the symbolism it carries. We associate crystal balls with magic and have for centuries. They feature in fairy tales and other stories—the kinds of tales that have always been the way we, as humans, have explained magic to ourselves. Peering into a crystal ball is participating in the history of magic and using the weight and power of that history to see further than we could otherwise.*

Once you've chosen the right medium for this particular scrying session, create a ritual space. Set up your mirror, candle, bowl of water, or crystal ball on a clean table, perhaps atop a sacred cloth set aside for this purpose. You can surround it with crystals that aid in divination, like lapis lazuli, opal, malachite, or amethyst. You could diffuse some essential oils like lavender or sage. Put on some music, or simply sit in silence, hearing the sounds of the world around you.

When you feel ready, stare into your medium. Feel free to blink, look away, or take a sip of water or tea. Gradually, you will find yourself relaxing into your meditative state. Don't expect to actually see anything with your eyes, necessarily—though some witches do! Most often, scrying is about looking *inside* and learning what truths are to be found within.

CREATIVITY SPELL

There are ways to work with runes or other forms of lithomancy that go beyond divination. One of the most effective ways to incorporate runes into your magical life is as talismans. You can purchase a stone or wood carving with a particular set of runes or Ogham inscribed on it—either for protection or balance, or whatever else you may desire. Or you can use thread magic.

Thread magic is one of the oldest and simplest ways to imbue everyday objects with power and intention. And you don't need to be a master sewer or anything; this can be extremely basic.

As always, start by setting your intention. What do you want to invoke? This particular spell is guiding you toward creativity, but you really can use it for anything.

Once you are clear on your intentions, choose your rune or runes. You might choose Raidho, to represent exploration, or Kenaz, for knowledge and inspiration. You might choose Inguz, the seed of creativity and fertility, or Laguz, for dreams, mystery, and imagination. Or you might use all of the above and more!

If you feel more drawn toward Ogham, you might choose Saille, the willow tree, for knowledge and spiritual growth, or Nion, the ash tree, for the connection between the inner and outer self. Or perhaps you will be pulled by Coll, the hazel tree, which is representative of life, wisdom, and creativity.

Sketch out the runes you want to use. Do you want them to overlap, or to line up one after another? This is your spell; be creative with it.

Once you've chosen your runes and their design, choose an object you wish to imbue with their power. It could be a blanket, something you like to curl up under, delightfully cozy, while you journal or write. It could be an apron, which you wear while you create food to feed your household. It could be a favorite top or an altar cloth. What object feels most useful to you in your creative practice?

Next, gather an embroidery needle and embroidery thread. Cut a length of thread that is long enough for several stitches, but not so long it'll tangle—eighteen inches is probably good—and tie off the end in a knot. Following your sketch, stitch your runes into the fabric. You can make it large and decorative or tiny and secret. It's entirely up to you. Again, don't worry—you don't need to be particularly skilled to manage this. It's about intention, not perfection. Wiggly stitches are just as powerful as straight ones if done in the right mindset.

INTUITION SPELL

Sometimes, you don't actually need anything at all to work with the Unseen—everything you possess is actually within you.

The third eye, called ajna when referring to the chakras or energy points within the body, is your connection to the Unseen, the place where hidden wisdom lies. Your third eye is located on the brow bone, between your eyes. There are several ways to stimulate or open your third eye, including working with crystals like lapis lazuli, azurite, fluorite, fuchsite, lepidolite, sapphire, labradorite, and apophyllite. You can literally place a crystal over your third eye chakra and let the crystal's energy begin to resonate with your own. It can also be helpful to anoint yourself with certain essential oils that resonate with ajna, including jasmine, vetiver, and rosemary.

But when you need to access your intuition and you don't have all your tools available—which is often the case, as we all lead busy lives and need internal answers right away—then *you* are all you truly need.

Find a bit of space, whether it's at your desk, in your parked car, or even standing on the sidewalk. Find a small bubble of space that is *yours*, for the moment. Close your eyes, and place the middle two fingers of your nondominant hand right over your third eye. Inhale and direct your internal gaze (your eyes remain closed) to the location of your third eye chakra. Focus on it. Focus on *you*, on your breathing, on your own internal experience that has nothing to do with what is going on around you.

Once you have established a clear channel between yourself and your intuition, turn your attention to the question or issue at hand. Let your answers flow through you.

SELF-LOVE SPELL

When we look inward, we often have a very difficult time finding things to love—even though that is precisely where true self-love exists. This is just part of the reality of being human in this day and age; self-love is hard to find. This has absolutely nothing to do with you or your own *worthiness*—it's simply that we are so often caught up in daily challenges and expectations that we let the best parts of ourselves become buried. The light can be as hidden as the shadow.

But here's the thing—even if it's hard to find, that self-love is always there. We always have the opportunity to be our own best friends. This spell is an exercise in finding that deep down self-love and working to bring it to the surface, where it can hopefully stay.

Start by doing something nice for yourself. Maybe that's lighting a scented candle or pulling on your favorite pair of socks. Maybe it's dressing in a way that makes you feel magical. When you're ready, pick up a pen and paper you can use for a practice in psychography.

As always in psychography, you are allowing the words to flow, letting out whatever comes. But in this case, try to focus it just a little. Keep it focused on self, and keep your energy positive. This can be quite challenging, but try to treat this as a gift for yourself. Allow kind words to flow.

When you feel complete, circle or underline whatever words or phrases feel truest and most nourishing. Sometimes, we need to be told we are kind or honest or generous. We need to be told we are good friends, lovers, siblings. And who better to tell us than ourselves?

Maybe you'll want to copy these words or phrases into your journal or write them on a card to place on your altar or beneath your pillow. These are your words, from deep inside of you, and they are true. Allow them to support you.

Light a Candle for...

MORGAN LE FAY

ARTHURIAN LEGEND, ~1100

"Morgan is her name, and she has learned what useful properties all the herbs contain, so that she can cure the body ills."
—**Geoffrey of Monmouth, "Vita Merlini"**

Legends of the actual historical figure King Arthur are so numerous and conflicting that it is impossible to determine which strands lie closest to the truth—and the same applies to his sister Morgan. Morgan was the daughter of Igraine and her husband Gorlois, but the wizard Merlin disguised King Uther so that he could sleep with Igraine, and thus Arthur was born.

Before the thirteenth century, the legends were much more straightforward and inspiring in general. Morgan was a witch related to Arthur somehow or other and acted as his magical protector and healer. But over time and as the stories developed, Morgan became morally ambiguous, and then eventually, by the time we get to Thomas Malory's *Le Morte d'Arthur* in the late fifteenth century, she was downright evil, matching the mores of the time that held that women who were powerful were therefore villains.

Uther gave Morgan in marriage to Urien against her will, but Morgan studied with Merlin, learning more of the magical arts, after which she was given the nickname "Le Fay." Eventually she returned to Camelot with her son Yvain to serve as an advisor to Arthur. There she took many lovers, including Merlin and the knight Accolon, but her affections for Lancelot were unreturned. She and Guinevere (Arthur's wife) detested each other, and so this may be the reason she cast a love spell on Guinevere and Lancelot, famously bringing the Round Table to ruin; according to some legends, this was intentional, as she hoped to steal Arthur's throne. In *Le Morte d'Arthur*, she stole Excalibur and gave it to Accolon; Arthur recovered the sword but not the healing scabbard, and so when he was injured in battle, he died of his wounds. In the end, Morgan was redeemed, and bore Arthur's body to Avalon where he could rest.

———◆———

Morgan Le Fay is one of those figures whose motives and even actions shift depending on who is telling the story. At her core, she is a woman who had power and the ambition necessary to use it.

Chapter Four

THE MOON

The moon is an integral part of all shadow magic. If we think of the sun as that which casts light, then the moon is its opposing force, a symbol of darkness and the unknown. The moon is mysterious. Often, though not always, the moon is viewed as having feminine energy, the yin to the sun's yang. Unlike the sun, which remains the same shape all the time, providing light even on cloudy days, the light we receive from the moon depends on where we are in her cycle. A full moon can seem almost bright enough to read by, while a crescent moon casts only a pale glow. A new moon isn't visible at all, but we know she is there, whole and complete.

The moon has a physical impact on the earth, as she literally drags the waters of our oceans for miles—and she has the same kind of physical impact on us. Our bodies, which are 70 percent water, are pulled and guided by her gravity and energy. Although there isn't really any scientific evidence for this, we often have trouble sleeping under the full moon, and when we do sleep, our dreams can be remarkably vivid and complex.

The moon has a mystical impact on us as well. She doesn't shine with her own light, but rather that of the sun, reflected and reinterpreted. Viewing things in her light can be like looking through a magical mirror—we see things distorted, but perhaps in that distortion, we can gain a better understanding. The moon's reflected light helps us to tap into our intuition and our creativity, unearthing our innermost mysteries—which is what shadow magic is all about.

The Moon Throughout History

In cultures all around the world since time began, the moon has been a powerful force in shaping the human experience. Some of the earliest artwork we know of—the sketches of horses and deer in the Lascaux cave of France—include a constellation of dots that archaeologists have determined to be a cosmic calendar depicting the moon's journey across the sky. When that calendar was made 17,000 years ago, the moon was the only real source of light after the sun went down. No wonder it was so important.

And it has remained so, even as we invented candles, then gas lamps, and finally electricity. The moon *means* something to us as humans. And that's not only true for mystics and witches. Some of the most rational minds we can think of have been known to harness the power of the moon. For example, in the eighteenth century there was a dinner club known as the Lunar Society, which would gather each Sunday nearest the full moon and would journey to and from their meeting place using only the light of the moon. The idea was that the moon could inspire their conversations and debates—which took place around the subjects of scientific and social advancement. Members included philosophers, intellectuals, industrialists, and scientists . . . including Charles Darwin.

The moon is interpreted differently by different cultures around the world, but some concepts remain consistent across many traditions. In ancient Egypt, the moon was thought to be balanced atop the head of the god Khonsu, who was known as the "pathfinder," and would protect the deceased on the journey to the realms of the dead. Similarly, during the Bronze Age, Celts in Ireland carved a map of the moon into their tombs, which would be illuminated by moonlight, offering a path for the souls of the dead to follow.

Just about every culture has worshipped at least one deity with a relationship to the moon. The list of lunar deities is *long*, and these are just a few examples. We can draw inspiration from some of their legends and stories. You may find, for instance, that it can be fun to bring a deity into your practice. It can sometimes be helpful to invoke a god or goddess when you're working with shadow magic, and moon magic specifically, or you can simply consider how you might want to embody some of their characteristics (turn to page 46 for a refresher on the creativity spell on how to do this).

Abuk ✦ African goddess, patron of women and gardens

Artemis ✦ Greek goddess of the hunt and of the wilderness, protector of young girls

Chandra ✦ Hindu god associated with the night and with plants

Chang'e ✦ Chinese goddess of beauty and thoughtful decisions

Dewi Ratih ✦ Indonesian goddess of beauty and grace

Hina ✦ Hawaiian goddess of creation and motherhood

Mama Killa ✦ Incan goddess of marriage and menstruation, defender of women

In the West, we think of the moon as embodying mystery and romance, and sometimes as a transformational force—werewolves are triggered by the moon, after all. But in many parts of the East, the moon is a symbol of peace and prosperity. Today, families in China and other Asian countries still gather to celebrate a 3,000-year-old lunar festival, honoring the goddess Chang'e. Islam, Buddhism, Hinduism, Christianity, and Shinto all have facets of belief and lore that invoke the moon.

We are and have always been the moon's children.

The Moon in Astrology

The moon plays a particularly important role in astrology. Whether or not you are versed in astrology beyond knowing your Sun Sign, it can be helpful to understand how the moon impacts us—as understanding the influence of the cosmos on the human experience is what astrology is all about.

The moon plays two separate roles in astrology. First, it functions as a luminary (celestial object) that moves through each sign. For instance, Venus spends about thirty days in each sign as she rotates across the sky, bestowing her passion as she goes. The moon, on the other hand, is much closer to us and so spends only two to three days in a sign before moving on to the next. But though her time is brief, it can have an enormous impact.

In astrology, the moon represents pure emotion. She is spontaneous and instinctual. She helps us sort through how our inner world relates to our outer experience. She also rules the ebb and flow of our energy. So when she stops by for a visit in your Sun Sign, you can expect your emotions to run high, which can be challenging. You might be moody or restless. But you can also reap the benefits of a stronger intuition, a deeper way of understanding truths that may seem irrational on their surface. You will likely feel more creative energy and be more imaginative during this period.

Moon Signs

Then there is the second function the moon serves in astrology. When we are asked the question, "What's your sign?" the answer is generally our Sun Sign (i.e., the constellation that the sun was visiting at the time we were born). But that's not the only sign we have, nor is it necessarily the most important. There are actually three signs that make up a much broader and more complex picture of who we are, and they all three play together in balance. In addition to the Sun Sign, we have the Rising Sign, which is the sign that was coming up over the horizon at the moment you were born, and the Moon Sign, which is the sign the moon was visiting at the time of your birth.

Your Sun Sign represents the core of who you are. Your Rising Sign is the image you present to the world. And your Moon Sign is your inner, emotional self. So, for instance, if you're a Leo with a Pisces Moon Sign and a Sagittarius Rising Sign, then you are extremely fiery, and everyone tends to see you that way, even if you don't always *feel* fiery inside.

The Zodiac as Moon Signs

MOON IN ARIES ✦ *With Aries's fiery nature, strong emotions are a given. Aries will demand that their needs are met, and tempers will tend to run high. On the other hand, lunar Aries are expressive change-makers, who can and will fight with all that they have for what they believe in.*

MOON IN TAURUS ✦ *For Taurus, safety and security are very important, and so to soothe the anxieties the moon provokes, lunar Taurus will work hard to make sure their most basic needs are met—and met in excess, nearing luxury and decadence. A lunar Taurus likes to be surrounded by beautiful things in a space that is peaceful and soothing.*

MOON IN GEMINI ✦ *Lunar Gemini is the epitome of an ambivert. They are always in conversation with themselves about what they want and need. Do they need space and some time to be introverted? Or do they need to go out and be among others, sharing their bountiful extroverted energy? Lunar Gemini needs both and needs to be accepted in their contradictions.*

MOON IN CANCER ✦ *Cancer is ruled by the moon anyway, so if Cancer is your Moon Sign, we're talking about a lot of moon energy. Sensitive and intuitive, lunar Cancer is easily hurt and feels things so very deeply. They crave true connection and love to demonstrate how much they care.*

MOON IN LEO ✦ *Lunar Leo's passion flares brightly. Their love can be powerful, warm, and generous. But behind all that fire is some insecurity, and Leo needs to know that their love is returned—indeed, they need constant reminding.*

MOON IN VIRGO ✦ *Lunar Virgo can be so hard on themselves. They are anxious and self-critical, but if they can overcome that self-doubt, they will work so hard for the things they care about, making practical and meaningful changes in the world.*

MOON IN LIBRA ✦ *Lunar Libra has a tendency to put everyone else's needs first, and when it comes to addressing their own desires, they can be so caught up in people-pleasing that they can't make a decision. But if they can learn the importance of self-care, they can be incredibly balanced in their relationships.*

MOON IN SCORPIO ✦ *Lunar Scorpio can seem very intense, because they can see much more than others. Their intuition about other people can be nearly psychic. Because they feel things deeply, they can be unforgiving.*

MOON IN SAGITTARIUS ✦ *Lunar Sagittarius is an adventurer, and with the moon's emotional and intuitive energy, they are idealistic and curious, wanting to learn and enjoy all that the world has to offer.*

MOON IN CAPRICORN ✦ *Lunar Capricorn has just as many and varied emotions as anyone else, but they want to hide and protect them. They can be prone to self-criticism when they aren't achieving what they want as quickly as they think they should, but they also work well under pressure, never letting their fears get the best of them.*

MOON IN AQUARIUS ✦ *Lunar Aquarius is an independent freethinker, happy to be quirky and wanting to help others feel as free as they do. That independence can sometimes lead to a certain aloofness and a lack of close relationships.*

MOON IN PISCES ✦ *The dreamiest of all, lunar Pisces wants to change the world. They are empathetic and romantic and crave closeness and magic in their lives.*

Light a Candle for...

CIRCE

HOMER'S ODYSSEY, EIGHTH CENTURY BCE

So they stood in the gateway of the fair-tressed goddess, and within they heard Circe singing with sweet voice, as she went to and fro before a great imperishable web, such as is the handiwork of goddesses, finely-woven and beautiful, and glorious.

—*The Odyssey*

Circe was the daughter of Helios, the Greek god of the sun, and the nymph Perse. Separate from the powers she inherited from her mighty parents are those she developed for herself, including her vast knowledge of potions and herb magic, which she famously used to turn men into animals. She turned Picus, an Italian king, into a woodpecker for not returning her affections, and when Glaucus the sea god left her for a nymph named Scylla, she transformed Scylla into a horrific monster.

Frankly, none of this behavior was particularly offensive in the context of Greek mythology, but Circe was eventually exiled. She lived alone on the island of Aeaea, protected by friendly lions and wolves who may or may not have once been men.

Odysseus, one of the few survivors of the Trojan War, sought shelter on Aeaea for himself and his men. However, his men were less than respectful, and Circe turned them into pigs. According to some stories, she spared Odysseus for his intelligence and wit, and according to others, he took moly, a special herb, to protect him from her spells. Either way, they eventually became lovers. Odysseus stayed with her on Aeaea for a year, and she bore him two sons.

Before he left, she freed his men and advised him on how best to safely make it home to his wife Penelope. Telegonus, one of Circe and Odysseus's sons, went to Ithaca to meet his father . . . and unfortunately stabbed Odysseus with a poisoned spear, not knowing who he was. Telegonus, Penelope, and Penelope and Odysseus's son Telemachus brought Odysseus's body to Aeaea to be buried. There, Circe and Telemachus fell in love, and everyone lived happily ever after by Greek standards.

———◆———

Despite being full of heroic deeds, Greek mythology does not offer us many exemplary heroes and heroines, and Circe is no exception. However, in a collection of folklore rife with abuse of women, Circe is a force of nature. She longs for love and connection, and yet is sufficient unto herself, making herself powerful even in her solitude and loneliness.

Moons Through the Year

Like all magic, lunar magic can and should be adapted to whatever your needs might be—you are the creator here, and your intuition will always be your best guide. That said, there are some complexities involved in working with the moon that can help make your practice more specific and often more effective.

As the moon changes and shifts in tune with our orbit around the sun, she takes on different aspects—different personalities, if you will. These shifting aspects of the moon have names that have been passed down throughout North American history, including by colonial Americans and Native American tribes—specifically the Algonquin tribes ranging from New England to Lake Superior.

Historically, these names didn't necessarily apply just to the full moon, but to the entire lunar cycle. There is some variation in these names between tribes, and of course the lunar calendar doesn't exactly line up with our imperfect Gregorian calendar, which means that a moon may not always slot neatly into one of the twelve months. But this is enough to give you a general idea and allow you to play with which moon best suits your needs and desires at any given time of the year.

January—Wolf Moon

The howling of wolves is often heard at this time of the year, as they mark their territory and reinforce their social bonds. Perhaps you might consider doing the same. This moon is also known as the Cold Moon, and its arrival heralds a time to work on the warmth of your home and social circle, blowing life into their embers.

February—Snow Moon

Often the bleakest month of the year, when snow falls heavy and winter seems never-ending, the Snow Moon is also sometimes referred to as the Hunger Moon. This cycle is a time to focus on gathering your resources and nourishing your body and spirit in preparation for the coming spring.

March~Worm Moon

This is not the most appetizing or magical-sounding moon, but it is a powerful one nonetheless. Now the life-giving worms are emerging from their slumber, signaling that it is time for all of us to get back to work. Perhaps that is why this spring equinox is also known as the Crow Moon, with that bird's raucous cries celebrating the return of life to the world. This cycle is an excellent time to begin a new project.

April ~ Pink Moon

One of the first flowers to bloom in the spring is the blossoming phlox, and this moon celebrates their gentle flush. Also known as Breaking Ice Moon—referring to frozen lakes and rivers, not awkward party games—this moon signals that our struggles will begin to ease, allowing us to bask in our first successes. It is an opportunity to find joy in the little things.

May~Flower Moon

This is a cycle of great abundance, of joy bursting forth. Alternately referred to as the Planting Moon, it is a time to take advantage of all that has come to fruition so far, and to use those successes to lay the groundwork for the next round of personal growth.

June—Strawberry Moon

So named because of the ripening strawberries that are beginning to redden the woodland floors in June, this cycle is also known as the Birth Moon. Birth isn't easy—understatement!—but it is glorious and joyful. This summer solstice moon is an opportunity for you to push through something you've been struggling with, resting in the certainty that it will all be worth it in the end.

July—Buck Moon

Named for the sprouting of antlers of male deer, which naturally occurs during this time, this cycle is also known as the Thunder Moon. There's a lot of masculine energy sparking at this time, which you can use to really dig into the work and planning that comes along with forward movement and growth.

August—Sturgeon Moon

The sturgeon of the Great Lakes and Lake Champlain are rumored to be easily caught under the light of this moon—which is also delightfully referred to as the Flying Up Moon. All that work you put in last month during the Buck Moon pays off here, allowing you to soar and gather all that you seek.

September—Corn Moon

Here is an example of how our calendar can make things a little confusing—if the full moon closest to the autumnal equinox falls in September, then it is known as the Harvest Moon, and not the Corn Moon . . . but if it falls in October, then *that* is the Harvest Moon. So the power of the September moon can vary; if it's the Corn Moon, then it's a time of creativity in work; this cycle asks you to use all your intuition and internal guidance to uncover what you need.

October—Hunter's Moon

If this is the full moon closest to the autumnal equinox, then it is the Harvest Moon. But if it is the Hunter's Moon (also called the Migrating Moon), then it is a time to seek and explore, as you venture forth externally to see what the world has to offer. It is also a time to explore internally, to see what *you* have to offer the world. In the case of the Harvest Moon, whether in September or October, this is a time to celebrate! You have reaped what you have sown and should bask in a job well done, surrounding yourself with friends and family, as you enjoy one another's warmth and support.

November—Beaver Moon

Also known as the Frost Moon, this lunar cycle is when the beavers have retreated to their lodges and are preparing to hunker down for the winter's rest. Follow their example and wrap yourself in a blanket—both literally and metaphorically—to give yourself a well-deserved break. Take time away from doing, and simply *be*.

December—Cold Moon

The Cold Moon is also called the Long Night Moon, for it is during this lunar cycle that the winter solstice gives us our longest night. The Cold Moon is an opportunity for introspection, for looking closely at the parts of yourself that maybe you don't always appreciate. Shine a light on your shadow, and find the love hidden there.

Following the Rhythm of the Moon

Moon-based magic is all about cycles, tuning in to the ebb and flow, observing the wax and wane of energy. We all experience this, with hormonal cycles, cycles in our energy and productivity, and just general emotional ups and downs.

We often think of our periods of lower energy as bad times. Those of us who struggle with depression and anxiety might experience them more deeply, but the truth is that everyone has points when they feel less joy and less enthusiasm for life. As with all shadow magic, it can be helpful to shift your perspective on these periods. Rather than viewing them as something to struggle with, get through, or pretend doesn't exist, we can try to see them as times of rest. The period might be called darkness, yes, but it's one that can help us work through whatever we might have been unable to see clearly in the light. With rest and reflection, we can make ourselves available to energy and joy again.

The moon can be a helpful reminder that these cycles come and go without us exerting any control. They are simply a fact of life, inevitable. Each part of the lunar cycle contains magic that we can harness. It's just a matter of shifting perspective.

The New Moon

On this darkest night, all you need to do is rest. It's time to simply *be* in the shadow. There is no action, no manifesting, no *work* that is required of you. You are at that "low point," which, like any other point, is neither good nor bad. Without judgment, view it simply as a time to be whole and at peace.

The Waxing Crescent Moon

This is a time when the feminine, intuitive energy of the moon is just starting to grow, to come into her own. It's the very beginning of this cycle—which means it's a time to open yourself up to possibility, to the flow of new energy. Consider the following ritual activities to do just that.

+ *Take a cleansing bath—whether full body or just a footbath—on the night of the crescent moon, releasing all that you've been carrying from the previous cycle into the water as you start fresh. You might soak in Epsom salts, adding some herbs for cleansing like mullein, chamomile, tea tree, and lemon.*

+ *You might consider journaling about what you want to invite into your life with this new cycle.*

+ *Practice Ujjayi Pranayama, or "ocean breath." Inhale, then exhale as if you're trying to fog up a mirror, making a noise. Feel that tight constriction in the back of your throat. See if you can make that same sound on your inhale—it's supposed to be noisy! When you feel comfortable doing so, close your eyes and focus your attention until all you hear and feel is your breath. Ask yourself, what is beginning in me?*

The Waxing Gibbous Moon

It's such a delightful word, *gibbous*. It refers to that incomplete state of being—not a crescent but not yet full either. It's the moment right before the full moon, when we are brimming over with potential, like a cup of water that's so full it's just about to spill. The following suggested rituals can help boost your energy, urging you to do the practical work you need to support your magical efforts.

✦ This might seem counterintuitive for a collection of shadow magic, but this a good time to harness the energy of the sun. After all, it's not like the sun ever goes away or that we shouldn't avail ourselves of what it has to offer. The sun is a powerful energy-giver, and this gentle, childlike ritual can help you soak up all that energy. Go outside if you can, and if it's possible to see the moon—as we sometimes can during the day—give her a little wave, a little acknowledgment. And then, just—play! Run, jump, spin in circles until you fall down. If you practice yoga, you might do some Sun Salutations, or you might close your eyes against the bright sunlight and interpret that powerful play of light against dark—what messages are you receiving?

✦ Create a crystal grid that mimics the arcing movement of the moon—and the sun—across the sky. Include tigereye, pyrite, yellow jasper, sunstone, and peridot to boost your energy, and ground yourself with obsidian, hematite, bronze, and smoky quartz.

✦ Use some energizing scents like thyme or mint essential oil, placing them on either the soles of your feet or in a diffuser. Bring your two hands into fists and hold them one on top of the other over your solar plexus, your chakra of personal power. Begin Kapalabhati breath, or "breath of fire," by sharply forcing your breath out through your nose, so hard that the inhale becomes passive, pumping in and out. Feel your core power activate.

The Full Moon

At this moment in the lunar cycle, magic and energy are at their peak. There's so much power here—and yet, we are only halfway through. The full moon is a time to take advantage of the light she has to offer and really reflect on what feels true to you.

+ *To perform a lunar scrying spell, fill a bowl with water. If you can, angle the bowl so that the full moon is reflected within it. Breathe into the water, disturbing it a little and causing some ripples, thus imbuing it with your energy, your soul. And, with that distortion, look within. What do you see? What has been hidden from you? This scrying spell can help you shine a light on what you may have been hiding from yourself.*

+ *Brew a cup of reflective tea, with one teaspoon of a combination of yarrow, sage, mugwort, and lavender. Pour just-boiled water over your herbs, then let your tea steep for ten minutes, covered. As you sip, journal as freely as you can, writing down anything and everything that comes to you. Skip punctuation and grammar, and just let yourself flow. Allow the moonlight to fall over your page as you write.*

+ *If you often have trouble sleeping on the night of the full moon, take advantage of this time! If you find yourself awake, keep as quiet as possible, trying not to disturb the dreamlike state that exists on this night. If you can, wander over to a place where the light of the moon can fall on you, and just bask in her presence, her blessing. Let the mysterious and divine feminine power of the moon tell you what she wants you to know, even if it doesn't make sense to you just yet.*

Waning Gibbous Moon

We are back at that not-quite-complete stage, but now the moon is winding down. You could view this time as a lessening of energy, but you may also look at it as a time to *use* the energy you've received. There is so much available to us from the full moon—but it is, after all, just one night. It is in the nights after the full moon that we can take all that power and run with it.

✦ *Make a second crystal grid, this time focusing less on the meaning of the crystals and more on the fun and artistry you can put into your creation. The idea here is to draw power for something beautiful, so depending on the season, gather leaves, dandelions, thistles, cornflowers, violets—whatever is growing around you through the cracks in the pavement. Spread out your crystal collection and incorporate whatever speaks to you, whether that is agate, amethyst, aventurine, chrysocolla, opal, rutilated quartz, or anything else. Alternate your crystals with your flowers, creating a work of art that will inspire you.*

✦ *Again, depending on the season, see if you can go out and wildcraft a tea for creativity. Collect raspberry leaves and mint from the forest—selecting and washing everything carefully, of course—and if that's not available, use dried mint and raspberry, which will work just as well. If you're using fresh herbs, brew your tea with a quarter cup of each, bruising the leaves first in a mortar and pestle. If you're using dried, they are much more potent, and you'll need only a teaspoon or a tea bag of each. The raspberry leaf will inspire slow, patient growth, while the mint will give you a burst of energy and clarity.*

✦ *The waning gibbous moon is a time to let things percolate and unfold. So rather than setting aside a time to meditate on anything in particular or work on any sort of breathing technique, simply let yourself daydream. Let your mind wander, and rather than swiping left on the thoughts that come up, spend a little time with them. What is alive in you?*

Waning Crescent Moon

The waning crescent is a gentle, loving moon. Her energy is quite maternal, as if she were holding us safe as we look back and consider how this cycle has gone for us. We can release anything we have carried through that we no longer need, simply basking in her love.

+ *Treat yourself with a soothing balm. You can craft it yourself by heating a quarter cup of sweet almond oil over low heat, and stirring in one-quarter to one-half ounce of grated beeswax. Let them melt and mix together, then remove the pan from the heat. Add ten drops each of lavender, clary sage, and rose essential oils. Pour the mixture into a small jar and let it solidify before rubbing it over your heart, onto the soles of your feet, or on anywhere that needs a little love.*

+ *Crystal energy work during this moon is very simple and gentle. Choose your favorite crystal, the one you feel closest to—if that stone doesn't resonate at this time, then consider using morganite, malachite, or rose quartz—and cup it to your heart center. Let it warm to your body temperature, and hold it to your sweet heart, feeling the love you have to give and to receive.*

+ *Anoint yourself with rose and sweet orange essential oils, placing droplets over your heart, at the base of your throat, at your temples, on your third eye, and on the soles of your feet. Cozy up under a blanket and allow the sweetness of this moon to hold you as you let go of anything you've been holding on to, whether that is regret, jealousy, anger, or any other emotion that has done the work it needed to do and is no longer necessary.*

CREATIVITY SPELL

This spell incorporates a tincture. A tincture is a particularly potent potion. In this case, it harnesses the powers of a variety of herbs to promote vitality, energy, thoughtfulness, and most of all, creativity. A teaspoon's worth is all you need. You may want to brew this for use during the next lunar cycle, as it takes a month to steep.

Add a quarter cup's worth of the following dried herbs to a mortar and pestle:

- Caraway
- Mugwort
- Thyme
- Lavender
- Sage
- Yarrow

Bruise them in the mortar and pestle, breaking them up and grinding them into a rubbly powder. Add them to a jar and cover them with vodka. Close the jar and store it in a dark place, like the back of your cupboard, for one full lunar cycle, then strain through a cheesecloth before use.

Whenever you're in need of a bit of a creative boost, reach for this tincture. Before consuming it, set an intention for what you want to create. This doesn't need to be a specific vision for a painting or anything like that—although it can be. You can want to create an open frame of mind, a peaceful space, a loving relationship—with someone else or with yourself. Once you have set your intention, take your tincture—you can simply place a dropperful on your tongue, or you can stir it into a cup of tea or a glass of water. Then close your eyes to let it settle within you.

INTUITION SPELL

The moon has a powerful impact on the tides, and we can use the moon's pull on water to enchant it, infusing it with lunar energy.

First decide what phase of the moon best suits your needs and intentions. The full moon is frequently the most popular choice, but perhaps you desire the fresh, growing energy of the waxing crescent moon, or the settling, grounding energy of the waning gibbous moon. On the night of the moon of your choice, fill a bowl with salt water—if you can collect it from the ocean, that's great, but dissolving some salt into tap or distilled water will work just as well. Choose your bowl carefully: Do you want to use a white ceramic bowl to visually echo the moon? Or perhaps a clear glass bowl to resonate with the water?

Blow your breath across the bowl, sending your energy into its depths. If you like, you can drop a piece of paper into the bowl after inscribing it with a rune, a sigil, or whatever phrase your intuition guides you toward. Let the bowl rest overnight, soaking up the moon's energy.

In the morning, pour it into a jar and keep it on your altar or by your bedside, close by whenever you need it. You can anoint your temples or third eye, dissolve negative energy into it, or cook with it for a little kitchen witchery—the possibilities are limited only by your own imagination and intuition.

SELF-LOVE SPELL

With this ritual, we can invite and receive the blessing of the moon. This can be done on any night of the lunar cycle, though it is especially efficacious on the night of the full moon.

If it's available to you, step outside to stand in full moonlight. If that's not possible, simply stand at your window so that the light of the moon falls upon you. Wear a low-cut blouse or a robe that you can open—or if you want to embrace feeling wild and free, abandon your clothing altogether!

Allow the light of the moon to fall directly onto the skin over your heart. Feel the push and pull of the moon and allow your heartbeat and breath to come into resonance with it. Feel that sensuality, that feminine energy. Feel the moon's glow within you.

Rest in this liminal space of power and possibility for as long as you want. Soak up all that it has to offer.

And then, release it, sending all that power back to the moon to reverberate against her and then return to you, like a wave rolling in and out. Will you howl at the moon? Will you chant or sing or speak an invocation? What do you want to release?

Light a Candle for...

ARIANRHOD

WELSH MYTHOLOGY, ~300 BCE

"I am the guardian of the past, the present and the future life. I am the Silver Threads of the Rays of the Light."

—Trobar de Morte, "Arianrhod"

Another frequently disrespected witch of the Welsh mabinogi is Arianrhod, and her story is even odder than Rhiannon's. She was the sister of Gwydion, the magician-hero-trickster figure of Welsh mythology. Gwydion served King Math, who lived under a very unusual and probably fairly inconvenient prophecy: Math would die unless, whenever he was not actively engaged in battle, his feet rested at all times in the lap of a virgin.

From time to time a new virgin would be required, and at one point Gwydion suggested his sister. To test whether her virtue was indeed true, Math instructed Arianrhod to step over Gwydion's magician's rod—causing Arianrhod to immediately give birth to a young boy, Dylan ail Don, who fled to the ocean to live as a sea spirit. Arianrhod ran away in horror and humiliation, but as she ran a blob dropped from her body. Gwydion trapped the blob in a chest, where it quickly grew into a boy.

Gwydion brought the boy to Arianrhod, but she did not react as he had anticipated. Instead of welcoming her brother, she placed a *tynged*, or curse, on the child, declaring that he would never have a name unless she were the one to give it to him. Frustrated, Gwydion left but returned soon after with the boy disguised as a shoemaker. Arianrhod watched the child kill a bird with a single stone and commented on how he was fair with a skillful hand, Lleu Llaw Gyffes—thus giving him his name.

Arianrhod placed a second *tynged*, this time proclaiming that he would never bear arms unless she gave them to him. And again, Gwydion set himself to trick his sister, leaving and returning, this time disguising himself and Lleu Llaw Gyffes as bards. Gwydion spent the evening telling stories until Arianrhod's court had fallen asleep. While they slept, he conjured the illusion of a fleet of warships attacking, and then woke everyone with a warning. Arianrhod armed everyone present—including Lleu Llaw Gyffes.

Arianrhod placed a third and final *tynged* on her son—that he would never marry a woman of this world. In answer, Gwydion and Math created a woman made of oak blossom, broom, and meadowsweet, calling her Blodeuwedd, "flower face," and eventually she and Lleu Llaw Gyffes were married.

The trickery in this story is so obvious it beggars belief—do we really expect Arianrhod to not recognize her own child? Multiple times? But honestly, we needn't believe it. We can interpret this story as a woman who lacked control—being given as "foot-holder" to a king must be one of the most demeaning things to happen in all of folklore—taking charge of her life and the life of her son in the only way that she could. She made it so only **she** *could give him a name and so that only* **she** *could determine if he was ready for battle. She also forced her brother to create a wife for her son— though that didn't work out all that well for Lleu, as Blodeuwedd ended up betraying him.*

Chapter Five
DREAM MAGIC

reams have always held a certain power and fascination. What are they, after all? Sometimes they make sense—when we are feeling anxious and not in control of our own lives, we may dream of driving a car when the brakes fail or the steering wheel doesn't work. Anxiety dreams are usually fairly easy to interpret. But what about more complex dreams? Dreams of flying, of saving the world, of falling in love, of nonexistent lands of impossible beauty? What do these all mean?

Some would say that dreams don't mean anything, that they are simply our unconscious mind's way of working out the stresses of the day. But truly, what greater meaning could there be than that? As Carl Jung puts it, "The dream is a little hidden door in the innermost and most secret recesses of the soul, opening into that cosmic night which was psyche long before there was any ego-consciousness, and which remains psyche no matter how far our ego-consciousness extends." [1]

Jung was quite the poet for a psychologist. He believed that dreams were the most effective means we have for understanding our deepest, most hidden selves. That doesn't make them easy to interpret, though. Dreams often contain truths that we keep secret from everyone—including ourselves. But Jung would once again have us turn to symbolism and archetypes for understanding, for they are the language of dreams.

Of course, the problem with all symbolism is that it is slightly different for each person. The old woman who visited Jung in dreams meant wisdom for him, but for someone else, she might represent the Divine Feminine or witchcraft or ancestors—which are all forms of wisdom, in a way, but not quite the same thing.

The shadow appears in our dreams in a variety of forms, and it can take time to get to know and understand its presence there. That said, dreaming interactions with the shadow can be some of the most profound ways to interact with it and to eventually understand and integrate it into our everyday experiences.

Everyone's shadow presents itself differently in a dream. It might take a literal form, like a person with whom you can have an actual conversation, or it can appear

1   Carl Jung, "The Meaning of Psychology for Modern Man" (1933), in *The Collected Works of C. J. Jung, vol. 10: Civilization in Transition* (New York: Pantheon, 1953), 144–45.

as a certain mood that you can begin to recognize over time. Maybe you dream of yourself doing something truly terrible, like harming someone you love. That can be awful, but try not to be too hard on yourself about it; the dream is simply allowing your shadow to speak up about its hidden fears, resentments, and frustrations. That violence is simply how your shadow is expressing itself in the only language it has. One thing to recognize about dreams is that every single person, creature, or object in them is a representation of *you* in some aspect or another.

So how do we interpret the language of dreams, when dreams are by definition the most secretive and cryptic experiences we have? As with all communication, it starts with listening carefully. We can take the symbols offered by Jung and by various dream dictionaries and use them to do an initial interpretation of our own dreams. Keep a dream journal, pay attention, and most importantly, trust your intuition. It too speaks the language of dreams.

Dream Symbols

The dream symbols below are fairly common. Each has agreed-upon meanings derived from various cultures, religions, stories, and the myriad other ways in which we've made meaning of our experiences over time—though this list is by no means complete. Dream dictionaries can be as long and as detailed as any etymological dictionary. But again, these are just general interpretations, and each of these symbols could mean something different for you specifically. Pay attention to their context in your dream, as well as to how they feel when you think about them when you're awake. If you have a recurring dream, then you definitely want to pay attention to what it's trying to communicate to you.

Abandonment ✦ If you are abandoned in a dream, it may indicate that you need to let go of your attachments, whether to certain people or to certain ideas and attitudes. Dreaming of abandoning someone else may indicate that you are overwhelmed and need to let some responsibilities go.

Abduction ✦ Dreaming of being abducted indicates that you feel a lack of control of your own life, while abducting another person suggests that you may be holding on too tightly to a certain way of thinking or feeling.

Abyss ✦ Indicates fear of your own inner self, the unknown shadow.

Accident ✦ To dream that you are in a car, train, or other accident signifies a sense of guilt over an error you made or a fear that you are about to cause inadvertent harm to someone else.

Acorn ✦ Symbolizes strength, durability, and growth.

Actor ✦ Dreaming of a celebrity indicates certain aspects of this person that you already have or would like to embody.

Adultery ✦ To dream that you are cheating on someone doesn't mean that you will or even want to. It can indicate a self-betrayal or a stressful situation in your daily life. If you dream that you are being cheated on, it can indicate fears about a relationship.

Amputation ✦ To dream that you have lost a limb indicates that you have abandoned something important to you or feel like you no longer have access to a part of you. You feel frustrated and need to regain your power.

Apple ✦ Symbolizes knowledge, wisdom, health, and prosperity.

Asphyxiation ✦ Dreaming that you cannot breathe indicates a sense of feeling smothered, either in a relationship or another situation in your life.

Attic ✦ Symbolizes hidden memories or secret thoughts.

Bath ✦ Symbolizes a washing away, a cleansing of the self—may indicate that you are ready to offer or receive forgiveness.

Beach ✦ A beach can signify the meeting between two conflicting states, or it can also point to a coming transition.

Bell ✦ Hearing a bell in your dream can be a warning sign or a signal that something new is about to begin in your life.

Bird ✦ *Dreaming of birds can be symbolic of your goals and hopes, a sign that they are about to come true.*

Black Cat ✦ *A black cat may indicate that you aren't trusting your own intuition.*

Blind ✦ *Dreaming that you are blind suggests that you are refusing to see the truth of something in your life.*

Blood ✦ *A dream that features blood may be about your life and passions, the things that are most important to you.*

Bones ✦ *Bones are symbolic of underlying habits common in your family or culture; they can also indicate your hidden strengths.*

Bridge ✦ *Dreaming of crossing a bridge indicates that you are in the process of making a big decision or about to make a big change. If the bridge is over water, the change is likely emotional.*

Burial ✦ *If you dream that you are being buried, then you are likely feeling overwhelmed and trapped.*

Butterfly ✦ *If you see a butterfly in your dream, you are likely feeling creative and joyful, and perhaps experiencing a transformation or finding a new way of thinking about something.*

Candle ✦ *A lit candle is symbolic of knowledge and the search for truth, while an unlit candle may mean that you believe you aren't living up to your potential.*

Castle ✦ *Dreaming that you live in a castle may mean that you are feeling defensive or that you are valuing success too highly.*

Cat ✦ *Cats are symbolic of independence and feminine power.*

Cave ✦ *Dreaming that you are in a cave suggests that you seek protection; a dark cave may be symbolic of your unconscious.*

Choking ✦ *Dreaming of choking may mean that you are having trouble accepting a situation in your life or that you cannot express yourself.*

Cliff ✦ *If you dream of standing on the edge of a cliff, you may be reaching a new level of understanding—a new perspective. If you dream that you are falling off of the cliff, you are likely afraid of failing at a situation you are facing.*

Clouds ✦ *Symbolize peace and compassion.*

Cobwebs ✦ *Dreaming of cobwebs suggests that you are neglecting something important to you.*

Crossroads ✦ *Crossroads signify an important decision or a coming change.*

Crow ✦ *This bird can be a messenger, likely from your unconscious.*

Daisy ✦ *Indicates beauty, innocence, friendship.*

Darkness ✦ *Indicates ignorance , fear, secrets.*

Death ✦ *Dreaming about the death of someone else may suggest that you feel you are lacking something they have, maybe a personality trait. Dreaming about your own death may suggest that a change is coming, likely within yourself.*

Dog ✦ *Symbolizes loyalty, protection, and good intentions.*

Dragon ✦ *Signifies a strong will, and possibly a fiery temper.*

Dragonfly ✦ *Indicates change and regeneration.*

Drowning ✦ *Dreaming that you are drowning may mean that you are feeling overwhelmed by your own emotions.*

Egg ✦ Eggs are symbols of fertility, birth, creative potential.

Feather ✦ Can indicate ease, comfort, lightheartedness.

Fire ✦ A fire in your dream may represent ambition or destruction, or possibly creativity or desire.

Fish ✦ Dreaming of fish usually means that you are trying to understand your own emotions.

Flying ✦ Dreaming that you are flying means that you are finally feeling a sense of freedom.

Food ✦ May symbolize a hunger for knowledge.

Fox ✦ This wild creature symbolizes insight, cleverness, cunning, resourcefulness.

Ghost ✦ Dreaming of a ghost may mean that you are longing for something that is no longer available to you or that you are feeling disconnected from the people in your life.

Hands ✦ Your hands are symbolic of your relationships with the people around you.

Horse ✦ Symbolizes strength, power, endurance.

House ✦ Houses in dreams are often thought to represent the self, with each room serving as a different aspect of your personality.

Key ✦ Keys indicate opportunities, access, freedom, knowledge.

Killing ✦ Dreaming that you are killing someone may mean that you are worried about losing your self-control or that you are wanting to "kill off" an aspect of yourself.

Knife ✦ Anger, separation, or a desire to cut something or someone out of your life may show up in your dreams as a knife.

Knots ✦ Symbolize small problems, worries, feeling constrained.

Labyrinth ✦ Dreaming that you are in a labyrinth suggests that you are feeling trapped or that you are working to get to the bottom of an issue—to understand it.

Lavender ✦ Indicates mysticism, cleansing, calm.

Lost ✦ *Dreaming that you are lost may mean that you feel you aren't on the right path in your life or that you are trying to adjust to a new situation.*

Magic ✦ *If you dream you can do magic, then you may need to consider how you can use your power in different ways in your daily life.*

Mask ✦ *Dreaming that you wear a mask may mean that you are trying to be someone you are not.*

Monster ✦ *In dreams, monsters often represent aspects of yourself that you fear or find repulsive.*

Moon ✦ *Symbolizes femininity, intuition, mystery.*

Mountain ✦ *Indicates an obstacle, challenge, achievement.*

Naked ✦ *Dreaming of being naked means that you are afraid of being exposed, of losing control of a secret you are keeping. You may also be feeling vulnerable.*

Nest ✦ *Conveys safety, comfort, protection, new opportunities.*

Oak ✦ *Symbolizes longevity, stability, strength, wisdom, and prosperity.*

Postapocalypse ✦ *Dreaming of life after an apocalypse may mean that you are working to overcome a big challenge and that you need to be resourceful and independent.*

Pregnant ✦ *Dreaming that you are pregnant may suggest that you are nurturing a new aspect of yourself or working toward a new goal.*

Rabbit ✦ *Symbolizes luck, power, success, and fertility.*

Rain ✦ *Signifies forgiveness, grace, or possibly grief.*

Rainbow ✦ *Indicates hope, success, and good fortune.*

Raven ✦ *This bird winging its way into your dream can indicate a betrayal, misfortune, or perhaps the symbolic death of a phase of your life.*

Reflection ✦ *Your reflection in your dream represents your true, hidden self—with all its flaws and perfections.*

River ✦ A clear and calm river indicates that you are going with the flow, living peacefully. If you are crossing the river, then it symbolizes an obstacle you need to overcome in order to reach your goal.

Roots ✦ The roots of a tree may symbolize the core of your soul, or they may represent your values, likely inherited from your ancestors.

Roses ✦ Indicate love, passion, femininity, and romance.

Running ✦ Dreaming that you are running away from something or someone suggests that you are running away from something in waking life, as well—perhaps there is a truth that you are unwilling to accept or a responsibility that you are trying to avoid.

Salt ✦ Symbolizes truth, dedication, and protection.

School ✦ Dreaming that you are back in school suggests that you are working through some insecurities or some childhood memories are resurfacing.

Sea ✦ The ocean in dreams represents the unconscious and the emotions.

Shadow ✦ To see your literal shadow in a dream is to see your symbolic one or an aspect of yourself that you haven't fully accepted.

Shell ✦ Signifies shelter, protection, or possibly secrets.

Snake ✦ Symbolizes hidden fears, temptation, or perhaps sexuality.

Stairs ✦ Dreaming of walking up a flight of stairs suggests that you are learning something new or gaining a better understanding of a situation. Dreaming of walking down a flight of stairs suggests that you are going back into your unconscious and whatever thoughts or emotions you have not been paying attention to.

Stones ✦ Symbolize strength, unity, and permanence.

Storm ✦ Indicates a struggle, shock, or possibly anger.

Swamp ✦ A swamp in a dream may suggest that you are feeling overwhelmed or insecure.

Swimming ✦ Dreaming that you are swimming suggests that you are exploring your own unconscious mind and emotions.

Teeth ✦ Dreaming that your teeth are falling out suggests that you have said something you regret.

Test ✦ Dreaming of taking a test you haven't prepared for means that you are feeling anxious about a situation in your life or that you are feeling judged by someone.

Vines ✦ Indicate hope, ambition, exploration.

Waterfall ✦ Symbolizes letting go, particularly of pent-up emotions.

Wolf ✦ Signifies survival, solitude, or perhaps aggression.

Woods ✦ May carry the meaning of fertility, wisdom, or exploration.

Intentional Dreaming

Interpreting your dreams requires little more than paying attention. But you can increase your understanding of them by being a little more intentional with your dreaming—through connecting with your dreams and making them an important part of your life. Start by keeping a dream journal, a notebook that you store by your bed and use to write down anything and everything that you remember as soon as you wake up, while your dreams are most clear. Once you've written everything down, you can begin to process and work to understand what your dreams were trying to tell you. Pay particular attention to recurring dreams or even just recurring themes within dreams, including dream locations that may or may not exist in waking life. When you dream the same thing over and over, your shadow is definitely trying to get something through to you.

You can create more intention by committing to rituals around your sleep. Here you'll find one intended for before you go to bed and another for right when you wake up.

Pre ~ Dreaming Ritual

✦ Light a silver candle and do a brief meditation, letting go of the weight of the day.

✦ Spritz your face or your pillow with a gentle spray—one part water, one part witch hazel, and a few drops of lavender or chamomile essential oil (or any essential oils of your choice, whatever feels comforting and restful to you).

✦ Give a little tap on your dreaming spell jar (see page 138) as a little reminder to it and to yourself of your intentions for your night's rest.

Post ~ Dreaming Ritual

It can be helpful to mull over your dreams during your morning meditation or while sipping a cup of tea (see page 140). Write down any insights you find in your journal, and let your mind continue to ruminate over the course of the day. You don't have to sit there and really *think*. Simply allow your intuition and understanding to grow. Pay attention to the details of your dreams, including:

✦ Events, like whether you got lost or couldn't breathe, etc.

✦ Locations, including whether they exist in your waking life or only in your dreams

✦ Any emotions you felt

✦ Any people you interacted with, whether real or imaginary

✦ Any powers you had

✦ How you felt upon waking (rested, anxious, happy, etc.)

✦ When the dream occurred, including the time of night, the point in the lunar cycle, or under which moon or astrological sign (see page 96)

Eventually you will find that dream interpretation comes more easily as you become more fluent in the language of *your* dreams.

Lucid Dreaming

Once you have a handle on understanding your dreams, you can begin to control them. One step beyond intentional dreaming is lucid dreaming, where we don't simply *allow* and seek to understand our dreams but instead actively choose them. This isn't something you would want to do every night, as ordinary dreaming is an important way for you to look within and process the complexities of your life. But every once in a while it can be quite magical to explore this power.

To control your dreams, you need to be aware that you *are* dreaming while it is happening. The more you practice intentional dreaming, the easier this becomes, as simply paying attention to your dreams helps you become more aware of what a dream state feels like. Start by trying to recognize it and state to yourself *I'm dreaming* before attempting to change anything.

This is easiest in those moments when you're just barely drifting off, like when you're taking a nap or in the early morning hours. Once you notice you're dreaming, see if you can choose a direction for the dream to go. If it's a stressful anxiety dream, see if you can redirect yourself, perhaps by finding the hidden room you've been searching for over and over in your dream or by regaining control of a car you've lost the ability to steer. If it's a gentle dream already, sweet and pleasant, see if you can explore a little. If it's a heavily plotted adventure of a dream, see if you can make the story go the way you want it to. Lucid dreaming allows you to have agency in your dreams.

What do you want to explore?

Nightmares and the Shadow

It makes sense that we would most often want to turn to lucid dreaming when we are faced with a nightmare. Who wants to experience the terrors we often encounter while we sleep—and ones that can feel no less real even after we are awake?

And yet, nightmares are extremely valuable. They help us understand and process fears and worries that we aren't consciously aware of. Our worst nightmares—the ones that haunt us in our waking lives—are a direct line of communication with the shadow. As painful as they can be, these nightmares are also the best way to understand how to accept and integrate the parts of ourselves that we fear the most.

Instead of trying to lucid dream your way out of a nightmare—particularly if it's a recurring nightmare—allow yourself to get closer to it once you're awake. Journal about it, paying attention to the details, and spend as much time thinking about what it might mean as you would with any other dream. In some nightmares we are being harmed, and in others, we are the ones who cause harm. The first doesn't make you a victim, and the second doesn't make you a perpetrator—remember, everyone and everything in your dream represents some aspect of *you,* and your dreams are a way of helping you work out how to love and accept all the parts of yourself.

✦ *If you are being chased, who or what are you running away from?*

✦ *If you are losing control, who or what are you trying to subjugate?*

✦ *If you are being harmed or harming, what are you frightened of and trying to protect yourself from?*

Dreams aren't always about what they appear to be. That's what gives them magic—whether for their ability to enchant us or their ability to reveal the deepest parts of ourselves. Take a look under the surface to determine what your dream is trying to tell you. It may well be something you already know but haven't wanted to accept.

This is difficult work, but it can be so valuable. Understanding ourselves with complete love and acceptance is the most powerful magic we are capable of.

Light a Candle for...

MEDEA

HESIOD'S THEOGONY, ~700 BCE

"Of all creatures that can feel and think, we women are the worst-treated things alive."

—Euripides, *Medea*

Medea was the daughter of Aeëtes and the niece of Circe, and like her aunt, she wielded powers derived entirely from her own skill. She first appeared as a helper-maiden, supporting Jason and the Argonauts in their quest for the Golden Fleece so that Jason could claim his rightful throne on Ioclos from King Pelias. Aeëtes was in possession of the Golden Fleece and assigned Jason a variety of tasks.

By all accounts, Jason would not have succeeded without Medea's help. When he had to yoke flame-breathing oxen, she made him an unguent to protect him from their fire. She made a sleeping potion and drugged a dragon so that Jason could steal the Golden Fleece . . . and then, when Aeëtes would have stopped them, Medea killed her own brother Absyrtus to cause a distraction, allowing their escape.

They fled to Aeaea, seeking the protection of Medea's aunt Circe. Circe cleansed Medea of her brother's murder, removing the stain on her soul. At some point, Medea bore Jason children. Then, they left for Ioclos, but predictably, King Pelias refused to give Jason the throne, even though he delivered the Golden Fleece as promised. And so Medea arranged Pelias's murder, tricking his daughters into killing him, after which Jason and Medea fled again, this time to Corinth.

And there this already bloodthirsty love story went awry. Despite all that Medea had done for him, Jason still did not have a throne and still wanted one. King Creon of Corinth had a daughter named Glauce, but no sons, and so Jason married Glauce, though Medea and their children were right there with him.

The most famous version of Medea's story is the play by Euripides, even if for the 500 years before that, her tale had played out slightly differently. According to Euripides, after poisoning Glauce and Creon with a golden dress, Medea murdered her own children to cause Jason pain, though earlier accounts indicated that their deaths were accidental. Either way, despite her brother's murder, she had the support of her grandfather Helios, the sun god, and left Corinth in his golden chariot.

———◆———

Medea is the avatar of scorned women. She is depicted as jealous and vindictive, and no matter which version we believe—Euripides's story or everyone else's—she certainly killed without compunction. But then, so did everyone else in Greek mythology. The difference with Medea, as with Circe, is that she was a woman, and she killed with magic, rather than with a sword.

CREATIVITY SPELL

To support the creativity of your lucid dreaming, consider making a spell jar to keep by your bed while you sleep. Spell jars are a form of folk magic that dates back to the seventeenth century, and they are essentially a physical representation of a spell. Your spell jar is something you'll want to refresh relatively often, depending on what recurring dreams you've been having and how you want to impact your own internal dream state. Start by considering what you want to bring to your dreaming. Do you need more peaceful sleep? More power? More courage? Or perhaps simply more understanding?

Into a small mason jar, put the following:

For peace:

a sprig of dried lavender, chamomile, or lemon balm

moonstone, azurite, clear quartz

For power:

dried mugwort, wormwood, holly, or calendula

opal, lapis lazuli, amethyst

For courage:

dried mint, cinnamon, or yarrow

amber, carnelian, garnet, red jasper

For understanding:

dried marjoram, rose, or sage

rose quartz, turquoise, malachite

Consider your intentions for your dreams as you add each item to the jar, imbuing it with your own energy, power, and desires. Take a piece of paper and write out your intention, being as specific as possible. Fold the paper three times—or any other number that feels right to you—and then place it in the jar.

If there are any items specific to your intention, like a touchstone you've used, add it to the jar as well. Sprinkle a little salt over everything, then seal the jar tightly. Anoint it with a little essential oil, using the following:

For peace:
lavender or chamomile

For power:
frankincense or ginger

For courage:
myrrh, cinnamon, or sweet orange

For understanding:
rose, sage, or bergamot

Place your jar next to your bed, allowing its energy to work on you while you sleep.

INTUITION SPELL

If you're struggling to understand what your dream is trying to tell you, this tea can help boost your intuition and assist you in divining what messages you are meant to receive. Collect one teaspoon's worth of the following dried herbs in a mortar and pestle:

- ✦ Lavender
- ✦ Wormwood
- ✦ Yarrow
- ✦ Mint
- ✦ Mugwort
- ✦ Calendula
- ✦ Rosemary

Bruise them all together, mixing and blending them. Then tip the mixture into a tea strainer. Pour just-boiled water over it, then allow your tea to steep, covered, for five minutes. While you're waiting, gather your journal, light a candle, get yourself a blanket—whatever you need to make yourself feel comfortable and supported. When your tea is ready, feel free to stir in a little honey and milk, as it's likely to be a little bitter and there's no need to do magic that isn't enjoyable.

Sip your tea slowly. It will help open up your mind, allowing in messages that perhaps you haven't quite wanted to receive. Let your intuition speak to you.

SELF-LOVE SPELL

It's important, when working with dream magic, to make time for proper self-care—and it's *especially* important when dealing with nightmares.

When you're struggling to process a nightmare, this spell can help. You can do it when you wake up in the middle of the night if you want, or you can save it for the next day when you're feeling a little calmer.

Fill a bath—either a full tub or a footbath, depending on what's available to you—with water that is hot but not painfully so; you want this to be comforting. Add a quarter cup of the following mixture, storing the remainder in a jar for later use:

+ 1 cup Epsom salts
+ 1 cup baking soda
+ ½ cup dried rose petals
+ 20 drops rose essential oil

If you want to journal while you soak, processing your nightmare and working to understand its messages, do so—or if you'd rather wait until you've cleansed the nightmare a little, that's okay, too. When you emerge from the bath, you'll have drained away some of the toxins from your dream, but you can still use a little kindness. Nourish your skin with a few drops of the following, again storing the remainder in a jar for later use:

+ ½ cup almond oil
+ 2 tablespoons jojoba oil
+ 20 drops rose essential oil

Massage the oil into your feet, your arms, your legs, and over your heart, soothing your skin and muscles and being tender and loving to yourself. You are hurting inside, but you are loved.

Light a Candle for...

LILITH

ALPHABET OF BEN SIRA, ~800 CE

"And still she sits, young while the earth is old and, subtly of herself contemplative, draws men to watch the bright net she can weave, till heart and body and life are in its hold."

—Dante Gabriel Rossetti, "Lilith"

Once despised as the first earthly demon and now celebrated as a symbol of feminist freedom, Lilith has been a source of fascination. She was first mentioned as a primordial she-demon in Mesopotamian and Judaic mythology dating back to around 300 CE, but it wasn't until the early Middle Ages that the story evolved to reflect what we now understand to be her history.

As this story goes, in the Garden of Eden, God created Adam and Lilith at the same time from the same soil. Adam and Lilith were happy for a time, until conflict arose over which of them was the dominant member of the couple—explicitly when it came to sex. They fought and fought, and eventually Lilith left Adam and the Garden of Eden. She spoke the Name of God—said to bestow great power—and flew into the air. She made her new home in the Sea of Reeds, the place where, incidentally, the Hebrews would one day go to be free from slavery, mirroring Lilith's own flight.

Adam begged God for a new wife, and determined to avoid a repeat of the same mistakes, God took Adam's rib and made Eve from his flesh so that there was no longer any question about who was dominant. Adam and Eve carried on populating the earth—and getting themselves kicked out of Eden. Lilith went on to have her own children, perhaps sired by the archangel Samael, and her demonic offspring are known as the incubi and succubi—male and female demons of seduction.

───◄ ✦ ►───

*While the legend of Lilith served as a source of terror for prospective and new parents, she has since claimed her title of feminist icon. **Lilith** translates loosely to "the night," and she embodies all aspects of that—fear, but also sensuality and freedom. This First Woman, forgotten and shunned, refused to be repressed—refused to be second to anyone, choosing her own life and her own path.*

Chapter Six
PROTECTION MAGIC

Historically, so much of the magic witches have worked has been for protection . . . but protection from what, exactly? Certainly in Salem and Bamberg, witches needed protection from threats to their safety. And the history of magic in other cultures, including voodoo, is also a story of people in need of physical protection, but there are more ways to be harmed than just in the bodily sense.

Sometimes it's our energy that needs protection. While talking about your magical practice isn't likely to result in your drowning or burning, it can produce judgment. More and more people are beginning to understand what is meant by magic and witchcraft in contemporary society, but that doesn't mean *everyone* understands it. It's likely that there will be people in your life who don't quite get what you mean when you claim the title of *witch*. Family members and friends who care about you and mean well can still make you feel bad about the way you choose to live your life. Knowing that they can love you and still be incorrect in their judgment of you requires accepting all of yourself—which is what shadow magic is all about.

And, of course, there are other threats to our energy and sense of self, which come from everyday life. Every time you come into contact with someone else—whether they're a friend, a family member, or a person you pass on the street—you exchange energy. Sometimes this is completely fine, and you don't notice much of anything. Sometimes it can feel great, like when you have a pleasant interaction with a stranger at the grocery store. But sometimes it can be a drain, a pull on your energy that can leave you feeling uncomfortable or exhausted.

And it's not just other people who can affect our energy. Events in our lives, as commonplace as a bad news report or as pervasive as existential fears around climate change, are parts of everyday life that can drain us energetically. Those threats are real, and shouldn't be ignored. But we also can't be a support to those in need, whether they are close to us or across the world, if we are brought low as well. Protection magic isn't about avoiding negativity—this is shadow magic, after all, and sometimes there is value in the "negative"—it's about conserving our resources. It is our responsibility to protect ourselves so that we can continue to use our power, our magic, for good.

Protecting Your Space

The best thing we can do to protect our energy is to protect the space we live in. Our homes are meant to be a sanctuary, a place where we can heal, recharge, and feel *safe* in every way—including safe to be who we truly are.

Depending on your living situation, this may mean you can protect your entire house, or perhaps you can simply carve out an area that is yours and yours alone, a "room of one's own," so to speak. Once you have defined the boundaries of your proverbial room, you'll want to confirm those boundaries are secure. That starts by letting everyone know that those boundaries exist—if you're setting aside a room that is *yours,* make sure everyone in your household knows and respects that.

But, of course, you need to maintain the energetic boundary of your space as well. We can't keep *everything* out—even in the most peaceful of homes, we can hear noises from the neighbors, sirens, a loud radio . . . these are just the things that come with living among others. The goal isn't to eradicate such disturbances but to work to minimize their impact.

Salt circles are a powerful form of energetic protection, though they can be a little messy. If you're able to sprinkle your salt outside, walk the boundaries of your property—if you're not worried about damaging your plants. If your circle is indoors, simply follow the edges of your space. Whether you actively clean up the salt (inside) or allow the elements to wash it away (outside), the power of the salt circle will remain even once the salt itself has been swept away, though you'll want to repeat the spell every few lunar cycles or as often as feels necessary.

Your salt circle doesn't have to be a *literal* circle, as our homes and rooms tend to be square rather than round. Once you've determined where you want your salt boundaries to be, gather enough salt to make a thin, sprinkling line along the lines you've chosen. Pour the salt into a bowl to make it easier to carry, and then walk your edges.

As you do, scoop up a small handful of salt and whisper to it, setting your intentions for protect. You can simply say "protect," or you can recite "nothing may cross," or even "bless this house," that very common spell for protection. Scatter your enchanted salt as you walk, whispering and sprinkling, until you've covered the entire boundary. Pay special attention to any windows and doorways.

As tempting as it will be to sweep the salt up immediately, try letting it rest overnight, allowing the power of your spell to soak into your space. Then, when you are ready to sweep, work from the outside edges inward toward the center of your space, gathering all the energy together and then releasing it by whispering your thanks to your salt and then disposing of it in the trash.

Protecting Your Energy

Energetic protection is the most important form of protection, because threats to our energy can come at any time, from anyone or anything. You can brush up against someone in an elevator and feel the impact of their negative energy. You can get cut off in traffic. You can receive an annoying email at work. These are just a few examples of the unavoidable drains on our energy we encounter every single day.

It can be helpful to think of yourself as a bubble, or perhaps that you are surrounded by one, and each of these encounters is another bubble, bumping into you, threatening to burst through or bump you off course. There are a variety of ways to strengthen your bubble, which you can think of as your energetic barrier.

Crystals for Energetic Protection

Crystals can be *incredibly* useful when it comes to protection magic. You can keep one in your car to hold when you need its calming energy, or you can carry a few around in your bag so you have them close when you need them. You can keep one at your desk, near your bed, or anywhere else where it can be a support for you and your boundaries. The crystals most commonly used for protection and cleansing include the following:

Black Tourmaline ✦ For sealing your energetic boundary

Bronzite ✦ For strength and protection

Clear Quartz ✦ For healing

Hematite ✦ For grounding, protection, and closing your aura

Obsidian ✦ For protection from spiritual forces

Pyrite ✦ For defense, protection, and cleansing

Selenite ✦ For clearing and purifying negative energy

Smoky Quartz ✦ For focus and protection

BREATHING MEDITATION FOR ENERGETIC PROTECTION

That bubble visualization can come in handy in the moment, but sometimes when you've had a particularly bad collision with someone else's energy, it is helpful to do a more in-depth meditation to clear yourself out. This meditation is meant simply to ground and support you, to help you find calm when you feel a storm within.

Start by getting comfortable and giving yourself whatever support you can, whether that means lighting a candle, playing some soothing music, diffusing a calming essential oil—you know best what you need.

When you're ready, take a deep inhale, slowly, for a count of four. Hold it for a count of four, then exhale for a count of six. Try to feel the breath expand in your chest, as if your rib cage is growing in all directions, and then let it soften, coming back to neutral.

Eventually, this rhythmic breathing will grow natural, and you won't need to think about the count any longer. When that happens, imagine yourself seated beside a gently flowing brook. See the reeds reaching up out of the water, and feel the grass beneath you. Hear the soft chuckle of the stream as it rushes over the rocks.

As with every meditation, thoughts will have been bubbling up within you this entire time. Now, whenever a thought arises, consider it: Is it yours? Is it true for you, and a part of your energy, the magic that makes you *you?* If it's not, imagine placing it on a leaf and letting it float away downstream.

When you feel cleared, imagine the power of this peaceful place surrounding you, reinforcing your bubble, strengthening it. Take the clarity of the water, the life-giving energy of the plants, and the strength of the rocks beneath the stream, and carry them with you when you open your eyes.

Light a Candle for...

THE WEIRD SISTERS

SHAKESPEARE'S MACBETH, 1606

"For charm of powerful trouble, like a hell-broth boil and bubble. Double, double toil and trouble; fire burn and cauldron bubble."
—Shakespeare, *Macbeth*

The Weird Sisters have gone by a lot of different names. They are the three Moirai of Greek mythology, whose job it was to ensure that every being—god or human—lived out their assigned destiny. They are the Norns of Norse mythology, the three maidens who tend the World Tree Yggdrasil and shape the course of destiny.

In *Macbeth*, Shakespeare called them Weird, or *wyrd*, meaning "fated." And while on the page they are ridiculous and quarrelsome and creepy, they do in fact set the tone of the play as "fair is foul and foul is fair," and they do guide Macbeth to his wretched end. In the opening scene, Macbeth and his friend Banquo have come to the sisters for guidance. The Weird Sisters represent darkness and chaos, but in fact their only role is that of the witness—they offer advice and prophecy, but their prophecies are murky and can only come true after Macbeth acts on them. They tell Macbeth that he will be king, but that Banquo's sons will rule. Once Macbeth has planted himself on the throne, he kills Banquo to ensure his own line of succession, though he does not manage to kill Banquo's son.

Feeling uncertain, Macbeth goes back to the Weird Sisters for more advice—this time they tell him that he will remain king until he is attacked by the wood (i.e., trees), and not to worry, no man born of woman will kill him. Interestingly, Hecate makes a brief appearance— she berates the Weird Sisters, seemingly her underlings, for not having informed her of their contact with Macbeth, and she takes it upon herself to ensure that Macbeth believes himself to be untouchable.

So Macbeth rests easy, until he is attacked by a man *named* Wood using tree branches as camouflage, and is killed by Macduff, who, it turns out, was born by cesarean section. And guess what? Banquo's son inherits.

Apart from Hecate's spell, and despite all their cauldron stirring with eye of newt and toe of frog ingredients, the Weird Sisters do nothing to influence the course of events beyond giving true-but-misleading prophecies that Macbeth can choose to act upon at will.

The characters' misfortunes have cast their own shadow over the play itself in another example of self-fulfilling prophecy. Though *Macbeth* is by no means the bloodiest of Shakespeare's plays, either in plot of in performance, it is considered so unlucky that it is only ever referred to as "The Scottish Play," and if an actor must say the name for one reason or another, they must turn around three times and spit or perform some even more elaborate ritual. Rumor has it that this is because Shakespeare used the spells of real witches in the text and they cursed it.

⟶✦⟶

The Weird Sisters, Moirai, Norns, or whatever we choose to call them serve as metaphors for the unfathomable workings of fate, guiding us to make decisions. But we could just as easily call them our intuition or our shadow. Macbeth is certainly guided by his shadow self, and perhaps he would have done better to listen to what the witches had to say and then think more carefully before acting, using all of his faculties instead of simply following his darkest desires.

Protecting Your Power

Protecting your power is the natural result of protecting your energy, as of course, they are one and the same. But you can take this further by intending to boost your energy, your magic, your power, expanding and enhancing it, so that it can withstand whatever you may encounter.

In all likelihood, this isn't something you'll need to do all that often. Protecting your power is something that you'll want to work on when you feel particularly under attack, like when you're going through an unusually stressful time or when you're working on something big, whether it's a manifestation spell, a project at work, or anything that feels like it could use an extra boost.

Crystals for Power Amplification

These crystals are useful to keep nearby when you're working on a spell, and in the case of amplification, it can also be useful to put together a grid, adding a little intention and structure to the energy of your crystals, which helps them to come into resonance with each other. Collect nine—or another multiple of three—of the following crystals:

Agate ✦ *For courage, strength, and self-confidence*

Amethyst ✦ *To boost your intuition*

Aventurine ✦ *To bring luck*

Bloodstone ✦ *For courage and vitality*

Calcite ✦ *To amplify energy*

Chrysocolla ✦ *To tap into your feminine power*

Fluorite ✦ *To aid in concentration*

Jade ✦ *For ambition*

Lapis Lazuli ✦ *For focus and amplification*

Mookaite ✦ *For adventure*

Opal ✦ *For amplification*

Peridot ✦ *For energy*

Rutilated Quartz ✦ *To strengthen the will*

Sardonyx ✦ *For courage*

Sugilite ✦ *To help you engage with your intuition*

Sunstone ✦ *For energy*

Tigereye ✦ *To enhance your personal power*

Arrange your crystals in order of size, and then place the largest one in the center, surrounding it in a circle with the remaining crystals. You can vary them according to color, size, shape, or texture—as always, listen to your intuition, and use your intentions to help the crystals work together to support you. Leave your grid in place until your need for it has passed.

MEDITATION FOR POWER AMPLIFICATION

Light a candle, and diffuse some mint, frankincense, or ginger essential oil. Begin by sitting in front of the above crystal grid, if you've made one, or by holding one of the above crystals in your nondominant hand. If you did make the grid, take the center stone and hold it in that same hand. Then, touch it to your solar plexus chakra, manipura, the chakra for personal power and inner strength. Bow your head and breathe deeply, focusing your attention and breath on the place where the crystal touches your body. When the temperature of the crystal matches that of your body—when its energy matches yours—close your nondominant hand around the crystal, holding it within your fist but keeping it in place over your chakra. Bring your dominant hand to cup around your fist, so that they are both holding the crystal and holding and supporting you at your center.

This meditation begins with Kapalabhati, also known as skull-shining breath or breath of fire. It is a little challenging, but deeply powerful. Ordinarily, we inhale with intention and exhale passively, but breath of fire asks us to reverse that, as we force-fully pump out our breath and allow it to come back in on its own.

Keeping your hands where they are, take a deep inhale through your nose, then push out the air, still through your nose, in short, vigorous bursts, engaging the muscles beneath your fists, beneath the crystal. Allow the inhaled breath to come into you, focusing your attention on the exhale. Once you find a rhythm that works for you, keep going with it until you feel tired and your muscles begin to protest. When that happens, continue for three more pumping, skull-shining breaths, and then come to rest, closing your eyes and allowing your breath to deepen.

Extend your inhales, and extend your exhales.

CREATIVITY SPELL

It might feel odd to need to "protect" your creativity, but often it's actually very necessary. Consider when you're working on a new project or when you have a new idea and how feedback, even if it comes with the best of intentions, can be harmful. Sometimes that feedback doesn't even come from anyone else, but from within yourself, when your self-doubt and insecurities threaten to block you.

This entire book has been about how to avoid that, but the reality is that we will never be without our insecurities, not entirely—they are a part of us. And so this spell is for when you want to remind yourself that you are not *only* your insecurities and that there is so much that you have to offer.

This is magic-as-artwork, so gather some supplies. Use whatever medium you feel most comfortable with, whether it's charcoal, pencils, pens, or watercolors. Choose a space and get yourself set up. Remember that this isn't about perfection, it's about creation.

Turn back to page 68 and choose runes that feel supportive and protective to you and your creativity, like Uruz, Thurisaz, Raidho, Nauthiz, Algiz, Sowilo, Berkano, Laguz, and Inguz. Sketch them out. Explore creating something *new* out of them and bringing their complementary energies into one whole. Keep your piece of artwork nearby as a talisman to shield and inspire you as you work.

INTUITION SPELL

Just as we need to protect our creativity, we sometimes need to protect our intuition as well. This spell is intended to seal in your energy so that you can know what is coming from you and your truth and what thoughts and feelings actually belong to someone else.

It's a more intense version of the boundary spell used to protect your space—in this case it seals your aura, closing it against all invaders. Gather five candles and place them at the five points of a star—you'll want to make it big enough so that you can sit at the center, and you'll want to make sure it's safe and the flames won't touch anything. Use salt to draw a pentagram between the points of the candles, whispering your intentions for protection as you go.

Seat yourself at the center of the pentagram, being careful not to disturb the salt. Light the candle directly in front of you, and then use that flame to light the others, one at a time. Close your eyes and take three deep breaths. Imagine the flames from the candles reaching upward, like columns of light stretching up into the sky. Imagine the grains of salt floating around you, shielding you. The light and the salt merge into one solid wall, penetrable only by what *you* allow in.

When your wall feels solid, open your eyes. It is still there. Even as you blow out each candle, your wall remains, moving with you as you sweep up the grains of salt and protecting you throughout your day.

SELF-LOVE SPELL

As humans, we are so easily hurt. Not just physically, but emotionally and spiritually. And the worst part is that the people who have the most power to hurt us are often the ones we love and who love us.

Knowing that someone can love you and still be incorrect in their judgment of you requires accepting *all* of yourself. This is a portable spell that you can carry with you, keeping it close by so that you have it whenever you need it.

Gather the following items:

+ Rose quartz
+ Rose petals
+ A small object of significance to you, perhaps a stone you found or a feather or a piece of jewelry

Cut a five-inch square of fabric, large enough to hold all your items. You can cut up an old shirt that you loved and wore so often that it fell apart, or you can use a piece of velvet or wool—something soft and gentle and tender. Place your items on the fabric, gather the fabric together, and tie it tightly with a piece of string or yarn. Keep this magic bag with you, and it will support you wherever you go.

Light a Candle for...

HECATE

HESIOD'S THEOGONY, ~700 BCE

"And that distill'd by magic sleights shall raise such artificial sprites as by the strength of their illusion shall draw him on to his confusion."

—Shakespeare, *Macbeth*

Hecate is a mysterious figure of Greek mythology and bears a greater similarity to Baba Yaga than anyone else. For one thing, she is largely absent in legend, despite being quite powerful and influential. Like Baba Yaga, she is also unpredictable, a force for either good or evil depending on her mood.

Hecate was the daughter of Titans, born to Perses, the god of destruction, and Asteria, the goddess of oracles and falling stars. Even after the fall of the Titans, Zeus revered her, offering her gifts and sharing with her the earth and the sea and the starry sky. He would turn to her for guidance and would invoke her name, and she wished happiness upon him.

Every member of the Greek pantheon ruled over some aspect of life, but Hecate held sway over a wide variety. Because of how she survived and thrived despite the transition from Titan rule to Olympian rule, Hecate became known as a liminal goddess; she ruled over the crossroads, where one space became another. She could cross between worlds, moving just as easily from Olympus to earth to Hades and back. Her followers would pray to her to protect them in their travels—though again, she was unpredictable and was known to refuse her protection, apparently without reason.

Because she could travel to Hades, she became known as a chthonic or underworld goddess. She held the keys to unlock the gates of death, and in the first century CE, Virgil described the entrance to hell as "Hecate's Grove"—though he noted that she was equally as powerful in heaven. When Persephone was lost in the underworld, it was Hecate who guided Demeter in her search.

Hecate was also associated with plant lore and therefore witchcraft, and was said to have taught Medea, her priestess, although other versions claim that Medea learned her craft from Circe. In Apollonius Rhodius's *Argonautica*, Medea showed Jason how to appease Hecate by bathing at midnight in a stream of flowing water, digging a round pit and sacrificing a ewe, sweetening his offering with a libation of honey. Following Medea's guidance, Jason left without looking back and did not cast his eyes on Hecate.

Jason wasn't alone in this—descriptions of Hecate vary wildly. In some tales she was young and beautiful; in others she was old and haggard. She grew to become a threefold goddess with changing faces. She was the protector of warriors, athletes, shepherds, and children. The Furies, those winged creatures that punished wrongdoers, were her companions, and while Hecate was a virginal goddess, the Empusae are said to be her children—female demons who tended to seduce unwary travelers.

❖

Hecate can be thought of as the mother of all witchcraft; she was the first, and she held the respect of any who encountered her. She was powerful and intuitive, choosing only the path that made sense to her without regard for the rest of the Greek pantheon, to whom she owed nothing.

Conclusion

There is no greater power than the power of self-knowledge. Once we know ourselves fully and completely, in all our flaws and all our goodness, we not only know what we are capable of, but also what we can become. We are intricate and variegated creatures, and there is magic in embracing the complicated, sometimes perplexing whole.

There is magic in choosing what you want to grow and nurture within yourself. It is a great feat of enchantment to take in all the energy that flows to you—from society, family, friends, your own history, the history of your ancestors—and alchemize all of it into a force for good. The shadow is the source of some of our greatest strengths, and integrating it and harnessing its power can help us shine forth with gifts we didn't even realize we had, with magic and energy we were keeping locked up inside, shut away in darkness.

All magic comes from within, from whatever you carry inside yourself, but you can use the energy of the world around you to access it and increase your own power. There is *so much* available to you, and you should make use of it all—the many and varied powers of the earth, the stars, the elements, folklore and symbology, dreams and the Unseen. As you work to reveal and embrace your shadow, you grow more intuitive, more creative, and ultimately more magical.

It is only within the darkness that we can embrace the light, and we can only be whole—ourselves in truth—when we live as *all* that we are in our full potential and power.

Acknowledgments

When you have worked with the same amazing group of people for so many books, it can be hard to come up with new ways to express your gratitude . . . even though you actively feel more grateful with each one.

This book was an adventure to write, and I am ever thankful for the support of Shannon Fabricant, whose faith and thoughtfulness helped find clarity amongst the shadows. Thank you also to Ada Zhang, for offering her insights and perspective. Ashley Benning, I used to dread copyedits—and then I worked with you.

Susan Van Horn turns design into an art form and never fails to notice every detail. Amber Morris is the Queen of Swords of organization.

Amy Cianfrone, Kara Thornton, Betsy Hulsebosch, Elizabeth Parks, Ana-Maria Bonner, and the entire marketing and publicity teams—I'd be lost in the dark without you. Thank you to Kristin Kiser and the entire Running Press family.

Dave and Neil—you guys are my shining light.

Index

NIKKI VAN DE CAR is a blogger, mother, writer, crafter, and lover of all things mystical. She is the bestselling author of more than a dozen books on magic and crafting for adults and children, including *Practical Magic*, *Wellness Witch*, *Ritual*, and *The Junior Witch's Handbook*, and the founder of two popular knitting blogs. Nikki lives with her family in Hawaii.

Also Available from Nikki Van De Car

PRACTICAL MAGIC
ISBN: 978-0-7624-6307-7

CALMING MAGIC
ISBN: 978-0-7624-7046-4

POTIONS
ISBN: 978-0-7624-7873-6

WELLNESS WITCH
ISBN: 978-0-7624-6734-1

THE WITCHY HOMESTEAD
ISBN: 978-0-7624-7376-2

RITUAL
ISBN: 978-0-7624-8142-2